CALVIN ELLIOTT

USURY

A SCRIPTURAL, ETHICAL
AND
ECONOMIC VIEW

OMNIA VERITAS

CALVIN ELLIOTT

USURY

A SCRIPTURAL, ETHICAL

AND

ECONOMIC VIEW

1902

Published by

OMNIA VERITAS LTD

*Ø*MNIA VERITAS

www.omnia-veritas.com

CALVIN ELLIOTT

TO MY READERS

I beg the sincere and thoughtful consideration of this book by all its readers. Please follow the argument in the order in which it is presented. This is the way it developed in my own mind and led me, step by step, irresistibly to its conclusions. Do not read the closing chapters first, but begin with the *"Definition."* I believe every candid reader doing this, and having a logical mind, will fully and heartily concur in the condemnation of usury.

I hope these arguments will be fairly treated and justly weighed even by those whose interests seem in conflict. I have simply sought the truth, believing that "the truth shall make you free." It cannot be that this or any truth is in real conflict with the highest welfare of any man.

If any sincere friends of this truth are grieved that the argument is so crudely and roughly stated, I can only say in excuse, that, so far as I know or can learn from the great librarians I have consulted, this is the first attempt ever made to fully present the anti-usury argument, and I sincerely hope that others, profiting by my effort, may be able to make it more effective.

The Author.

CHAPTER I

DEFINITION

In the evolution of the English language, since the making of our King James version of the Bible, many new words have been introduced, and many old ones have changed their meanings.

In the nearly three hundred years the Saxon word "let," to hinder, has become obsolete. It was in common use and well understood when the version was made, but is now misleading. Thus we have in Isaiah 43:13: "I will work and who will let (hinder) it?" Paul declared that he purposed to go to Rome, "but was let (hindered) hitherto." Rom. 1:13. Again we have in II Thess. 2:7: "Only he who now letteth (hindereth) will let (hinder), until he be taken out of the way."

"Wot," to know, has become obsolete. Gen. 21:26: "I wot (know) not who hath done this thing." Ex. 32:1: "As for this Moses, we wot (know) not what hath become of him." Acts 3:17: "I wot (know) that through ignorance ye did it."

"Prevent," from its derivation and use, meant, "to go before;" now it means to hinder. Ps. 59:10: "The God of my mercies shall prevent (go before) me." Ps. 92:2: "Let us prevent (go before) his face with thanksgiving." I Thess. 4:15: "We who are alive shall not prevent (go before) them who are asleep."

Charity, which now means liberality to the poor, and a disposition to judge others kindly and favorably, was at that time a synonym of love, and used interchangeably with love in the translations of the Greek. This is especially noted in the panegyric of love, in the thirteenth chapter of First Corinthians, and faithfully corrected in the Revised Version, though some have felt that the beauty and especially the euphony of the familiar passage has been marred. But the word charity is no longer equivalent to love, in our language, and could not be retained without perverting the sense.

Usury, when the version was made, meant any premium for a loan of money, or increase taken for a loan of any kind of property.

Theological Dictionary: "Usury, the gain taken for a loan of money or wares." "The gain of anything above the principal, or that which was lent, exacted only in consideration of the loan, whether it be in money, corn, wares or the like."

Bible Encyclopedia: "Usury, a premium received for a sum of money over and above the principal."

Schaff-Herzog: "Usury, originally, any increase on any loan."

This was the usage of the word usury by the great masters of the English language, like Shakespeare and Bacon, in their day, and is still given as the first definition by the lexicographers of the present.

Webster, 1890 edition: "Usury, 1. A premium or increase paid or stipulated to be paid for a loan, as for money; interest. 2. The practice of taking interest. 3. Law. Interest in excess of a legal rate charged to a borrower for the use of money."

Interest is comparatively a new word in the language meaning also a premium for a loan of money. It first appeared in the fourteenth century, as a substitute for usury, in the first law ever enacted by a Christian nation that permitted the taking of a premium for any loan. The word usury was very odious to the Christian mind and conscience.

Interest was at the first a legal term, used in law only, and it has always been applied to that premium or measure of increase that is permitted or made legal by civil law.

In modern usage usury is limited in its meaning to that measure of increase prohibited by the civil law. Thus the two words interest and usury now express what was formerly expressed by the one word usury alone. Interest covers that measure of increase that is authorized in different countries, while usury, with all the odium that has been attached to it for ages, is limited to that measure of increase that for public welfare is forbidden by the laws of a state.

The distinction is wholly civic and legal. That may be usury in one state which is only interest in another. The legal rates greatly vary and are changed from time to time in the states themselves. If a state should forbid the taking of any increase on loans, then all increase would be usury, and there could be no interest; or if a state should repeal all laws limiting the exactions of increase, then there would be no usury in that state. Usury is increase forbidden by civil law. Separated from the enacted statutes of a state the distinction disappears. There is no moral nor is there an economic difference.

Blackstone says: "When money is lent on a contract to receive not only the principal sum again, but also an increase by way of compensation for the use, the increase is called interest by those who think it lawful, and usury by those who do not."

The moral nature of an act does not depend on the enacted statutes of human legislators, and the laws of economics are eternal. We must not permit our views of divine and economic truth to be perverted by this modern division of increase into legal and illegal. In order that the whole truth may be now expressed in our language we must combine with the old word usury the new word interest; then only will we have the full force of the revealed truth. "Wherefore then gavest not thou my money into the bank, that at my coming I might have required mine own with usury or interest?" It is rendered interest in the Revised Version.

Throughout this discussion usury is used in its full old classical meaning for any increase of a loan, great or small, whether authorized or forbidden by the civil state.

CHAPTER II

THE LAW BY MOSES

G od determined to deliver his enslaved people from the bondage in Egypt, and to lead them out to the land he had promised to their fathers. They had been strangers in Egypt; now they should have a land of their own. To them liberty was but a tradition; they should now be freemen. They had been a tribe; they should now be a nation.

God raised up Moses to be his special servant and the mouthpiece to declare his will. He ordered his marvelous deliverance from the river, and his training in court as a freeman. He then gave him direction to lead his people out of their slavery, and also divine authority to announce to his people the code of laws by which they were to be governed in their free state. Some of these laws were ceremonial, to conserve their religion, that they might not forget their God. Some were civil and politic, to promote the moral, intellectual and material welfare. All were in accord with the moral and religious nature of man, and with sound economic principles. All were suited to promote their highest good, and to secure them forever in their freedom and national independence.

The great basal principles of law are found in concrete form.

Human life is sacred as we find from the explicit laws for its protection. The owner of an ox was made responsible for the life taken by "an ox that was known to push with its horns."

A battlement or balustrade was required on the houses, very like our laws requiring fire escapes. The principle is the same.

The laws forbidding marriage within certain degrees of kinship have been copied into the laws of every civilized people. The laws for the preservation of social purity have never been surpassed.

The rights of property were sacred. Each had a right to his own. Theft was severely punished. "If a thief be found breaking up, and be smitten that he die, there shall no blood be shed for him."

Each must assist in the protection of the property of others; even the enemy's property must be protected. "If thou meet thine enemy's ox or his ass going astray, thou shalt surely bring it back to him again."

The laws for the relief of the poor were kinder and more encouraging to self-help and self-reliance than our modern poorhouses. Deut. 15:7-11: "If there be among you a poor man of one of thy brethren within any of thy gates in thy land which the Lord thy God giveth thee, thou shalt not harden thine heart, nor shut thine hand from thy poor brother; but thou shalt open thine hand wide unto him, and shalt surely lend him sufficient for his need, in that which he wanteth. Beware that there be not a thought in thy wicked heart, saying, The seventh year, the year of release, is at hand; and thine eye be evil against thy poor brother, and thou givest him naught, and he cry unto the Lord against thee, and it be sin unto thee. Thou shalt surely give him, and thine heart shall not be grieved when thou givest unto him: because that for this thing the Lord thy God shall bless thee in all thy works, and in all that thou puttest thine hand unto. For the poor shall never cease out of the land; therefore I command thee, saying, Thou shalt open thine hand wide unto thy brother, to thy poor, and to thy needy, in thy land."

These divinely given laws never wrought injustice. They protected life, purity and property, and required mutual helpfulness. They were given by the divine mind, in infinite love, to promote the highest good of this chosen people.

These laws of God, given by Moses, positively forbade usury or interest, and this prohibition was so repeated that there was no mistaking the meaning. Ex. 22:25: "If thou lend money to any of my people that is poor by thee, thou shalt not be to him as a usurer, neither shalt thou lay upon him usury."

This law is more fully presented in Lev. 25:35, 36, 37: "And if thy brother be waxen poor, and fallen into decay with thee, then thou shalt relieve him; yea, though he be a stranger, or a sojourner; that he may live with thee. Take thou no usury of him, or increase; but fear thy God; that thy brother may live with thee. Thou shalt not give him thy money upon usury, or lend him thy victuals for increase."

Prof. George Bush makes the following note upon this passage: "The original term 'Neshek' comes from the verb 'Nashak' (to bite), mostly applied to the bite of a serpent; and probably signifies biting usury, so called perhaps because it resembled the bite of a serpent; for as this is often so small as to be scarcely perceptible at first, yet the venom soon spreads and diffuses itself till it reaches the vitals, so the increase of usury, which at first is not perceived, at length grows so much as to devour a man's substance."

An effort is sometimes made to limit the application of these laws by placing special emphasis on the poverty of the borrowers and to confine the prohibition of usury to loans to the poor to meet the necessaries of life; and it is claimed that the laws are not intended to prohibit usury on a loan which the borrower secures as capital for a business.

In reply it can be said:

19

1. There may be more benevolence in a loan to enable a brother to go into business than in a loan to supply his present needs. It may be less benevolent and less kind to lend a dollar to buy flour for present use than to lend a dollar to buy a hoe with which to go into business and earn the flour. The highest philanthropy supplies the means and opportunities for self-help.

2. A desire for capital to promote a business to gain more than is necessary to nourish the physical and mental manhood is not justified nor encouraged anywhere in the Word. There is just a sufficiency of food necessary to the highest physical condition. There is just a sufficiency of material wealth necessary to the development of the noblest manhood. More decreases physical and mental vigor and degrades the whole man. To seek more is of the nature of that "covetousness which is idolatry." Prov. 23:4: "Labor not to be rich." Prov. 28:20: "He that maketh haste to be rich shall not be innocent."

Riches are a gift of God and a reward of righteousness.

Prov. 22:4: "The reward of humility and the fear of the Lord are riches and honor and life." Psalm 112:1, 3: "Blessed is the man that feareth the Lord, that delighteth greatly in his commandments. * * * Wealth and riches shall be in his house."

"In the fourth petition of the Lord's prayer (which is: Give us this day our daily bread) we pray, That of God's free gift, we may receive a competent portion of the good things of this life and enjoy his blessing with them."

3. If the prohibition is applicable only when the borrower is poor it would be difficult to properly apply it by drawing the line between the rich and the poor. Many who are rich feel that they are poor and there are many high spirited poor who will not admit their poverty. Many rich live in conditions that some poor would call poverty. The line must be vague and indefinite

and always offensive. If any one should endeavor to clearly mark and emphasize such a division in any modern community he would receive the contempt of all right thinking people.

4. The laws of the Hebrews did not discriminate classes except in their ceremonial and forms of worship. There was but one law and that applicable to all alike. Even the stranger was included in the uniformity of the law. Num. 15:15, 16: "One ordinance shall be both for you of the congregation and also for the stranger that sojourneth with you, * * * one law and one manner shall be for you and for the stranger that sojourneth with you."

5. In the Hebrew community the man of independent resources did not compromise his freedom by becoming indebted to another. Debt was a sure indication of some embarrassment or strait. The mention of the poverty of the possible debtor is not to limit the application of the law but describes the borrower. Thou shalt not lend upon usury to the poor unfortunate fellow who is compelled to ask a loan.

6. The laws of the Hebrew state were for the promotion of equity between man and man and also for the protection of the weak and the helpless. With these objects all good governments must be in harmony. They can only be secured by general laws. It would be very imperfect protection to the helpless poor if it was permitted to charge usury to the covetous, greedy fellow who having much, yet desired to gain more and was bidding urgently for the very loan the unfortunate brother needed. Also even equity between the borrower and the lender would work a hardness in the conditions of the poor man. Full protection requires a law of general application.

7. Independence, self-reliance, self-support, was the condition aimed at and encouraged in the Hebrew state. Borrowing was only in time of sore need. The man who went a-borrowing was second only to the man who went a-begging. The brother who,

through misfortune became dependent, was able the sooner to repay his loan and return to independence and to self support.

8. In the repetition of the law in Deut. 23:19, 20, there is no reference to the poverty of the borrower and it cannot by fair interpretation be limited to the poor. "Thou shalt not lend upon usury to thy brother; usury of money, usury of victuals, usury of anything that is lent upon usury. Unto a stranger thou mayest lend upon usury; but unto thy brother thou shalt not lend upon usury: that the Lord thy God may bless thee in all that thou settest thine hand to do in the land whither thou goest to possess it."

CHAPTER III

USURY AND "THE STRANGER"

D eut. 23:19, 20: "Thou shalt not lend upon usury to thy brother; usury of money, usury of victuals, usury of anything that is lent upon usury. Unto a stranger thou mayest lend upon usury; but unto thy brother thou shalt not lend upon usury: that the Lord thy God may bless thee in all that thou settest thine hand to in the land whither thou goest to possess it."

While there is no reference to poverty in this passage and the prohibition cannot fairly be limited to loans to the poor, a shadow of permission to exact usury is found in the clause: "unto a stranger thou mayest lend upon usury."

Hebrews, who have been anxious to obey the letter of the Mosaic law, while indifferent to its true spirit, have construed this into a permission to exact usury of all Gentiles. Christian apologists for usury, who have not utterly discarded all laws given by Moses as effete and no longer binding, have tried hard to show that this clause authorizes the general taking of interest. To do this it is wrested from its natural connection, and the true historic reference is ignored.

Three classes of persons, that were called strangers, may be noted for the purpose of presenting the true import of this passage.

1. Those were called strangers who were not of Hebrew blood, but were proselytes to the Hebrew faith and had cast their lot with them. They were mostly poor, for not belonging to any of the families of Jacob, they had no landed inheritance. The gleanings of the field and the stray sheaf were left for the fatherless, the poor, and these proselyted strangers. But they were to be received in love, and treated in all respects as those born of their own blood. Ex. 12:48, 49: "And when a stranger shall sojourn with thee, and will keep the passover to the Lord, let all his males be circumcized, and then let him come near and keep it; and he shall be as one that is born in the land: for no uncircumcized person shall eat thereof. One law shall be to him that is home born, and unto the stranger that sojourneth among you."

Lev. 24:22: "Ye shall have one manner of law, as well for the stranger, as for one of your own country: for I am the Lord your God."

Num. 9:14: "And if a stranger shall sojourn among you, and will keep the passover unto the Lord; according to the ordinance of the passover, and according to the manner thereof, so shall he do: ye shall have one ordinance both for the stranger, and for him that was born in the land."

Num. 15:15, 16: "One ordinance shall be both for you of the congregation, and also for the stranger that sojourneth with you, an ordinance forever in your congregations: as ye are, so shall the stranger be before the Lord. One law and one manner shall be for you, and for the stranger that sojourneth with you."

Of these strangers it is explicitly said they are to be treated precisely as brethren of their own blood.

Lev. 25:35, 36: "And if thy brother be waxen poor, and fallen in decay with thee, then thou shalt relieve him: yea, though he be a *stranger*, or a sojourner; that he may live with thee. Take thou no usury of him, or increase: but fear thy God; that thy brother may live with thee."

2. There was also another class of strangers, including all the nations that were not of Hebrew blood, by which they were surrounded. These traded with them and often sojourned for a more or less extended period among them for merely secular purposes, but never accepted their faith. For this reason they were often called sojourners. With us, in law, the former strangers would be known as "naturalized citizens," these as "denizens," residents in a foreign land for secular purposes. These denizens were to be dealt with justly, to be treated kindly and even with affection, remembering their long sojourn as strangers in Egypt. Ex. 22:21: "Thou shalt neither vex a stranger, nor oppress him: for ye were strangers in the land of Egypt."

Ex. 23:9: "Also thou shalt not oppress a stranger: for ye know the heart of a stranger, seeing ye were strangers in the land of Egypt."

They were "denizens," but not citizens of Egypt four hundred years.

Lev. 19:33, 34: "And if a stranger sojourn with thee in your land, ye shall not vex him. But the stranger that dwelleth with you shall be unto you as one born among you, and thou shalt love him as thyself; for ye were strangers in the land of Egypt: I am the Lord your God."

This class of denizens or sojourners was also to be treated with the same kindness as their own blood.

Lev. 25:35, 36: "And if thy brother be waxen poor, and fallen in decay with thee, then thou shalt relieve him: yea, though he be a stranger, or a *sojourner*, that he may live with thee. Take thou no usury of him, or increase: but fear thy God: that thy brother may live with thee."

The sojourner or denizen is here distinguished from the stranger who had been naturalized, adopting their faith.

3. There was another class called strangers. This class was limited to the inhabitants of their promised land.

Robinson's Bible Encyclopedia says, on this clause: "'Unto a stranger thou mayest lend upon usury.' In this place God seems to tolerate usury toward strangers: that is the Canaanites and other people devoted to subjection, but not toward such strangers against whom the Hebrews had no quarrel. To exact usury is here, according to Ambrose, an act of hostility. It was a kind of waging war with the Canaanites and ruining them by means of usury."

God withheld his chosen people from taking possession of the promised land until "their iniquity was full" and the divine sentence of condemnation had been pronounced against them. They were to be rooted out of the land and utterly destroyed for their sins, and their land given to the chosen people. God declared that he would execute his sentence, driving them out before them, as his people should increase and be able to occupy the land. Ex. 23:23, 28-32: "For mine angel shall go before thee, and bring thee in unto the Amorites, and the Jebusite, and I will cut them off. And I will send hornets before thee, which shall drive out the Hivites, the Canaanite, and the Hittite, from before thee. I will not drive them out from before thee in one year; lest the land become desolate and the beasts of the field multiply against thee. By little and little I will drive them out from before thee, until thou be increased, and inherit the land. And I will set my bounds from the Red Sea even unto the sea of the Philistines, and from the desert unto the river: for I will deliver the inhabitants of the land into your hand; and thou shalt drive them out before thee. Thou shalt make no covenant with them, nor with their gods."

Ex. 34:10-12: "And he said, Behold, I make a covenant: before all thy people I will do marvels, such as have not been done in all the earth, nor in any nation: and all the people among which thou art shall see the work of the Lord: for it is a terrible thing that I will do with thee. Observe thou that which I command thee this day: behold, I drive out before thee the Amorite, and the Canaanite, and the Hittite, and the Perizzite, and the Hivite, and the Jebusite. Take heed to thyself, lest thou make a covenant with the inhabitants of the land whither thou goest, lest it be for a snare in the midst of thee."

They were in no way to covenant with this people and interfere with the execution of divine judgment. They were commanded, willing or unwilling, to be in a measure the executioners of those under sentence. These people of Canaan were deprived of all rights by the divine sentence and the Israelites were not to grant any. To do so was direct disobedience, and yet most of the tribes failed to obey the command, permitting many of the inhabitants to remain.

When the Gibeonites deceived Joshua and secured a pledge, the pledge of their lives was kept, but they were made slaves, doomed to drudgery forever, "hewers of wood and drawers of water." Josh. 9:23.

This compromise was contrary to the divine command for their utter destruction. To condone the guilt of these people, or to interfere with their execution, was as flagrant a violation of law as that of a modern community that seeks to protect criminals, or that interferes with the execution of those convicted of capital crimes.

This class of strangers had no rights that Hebrews were permitted to respect. They were not to be given any privileges.

They were to be treated as Hindoo widows are treated, "accursed of the gods and hated of men." Debts were not to be forgiven them. The year of Jubilee did not affect them. They remained enslaved forever. The Sabbath's rest was only incidental, that there might be a complete cessation of all activities.

In the fourth commandment Deut. 5:14, "thy stranger" is mentioned after the ox, ass, and cattle, and was given rest for the same reason the beasts are permitted to rest: "That thy man-servant and maid-servant may rest as well as thou." They had not the rights of a common servant or slave. The carcass of the animal that died of itself could be given them to eat, and they could be charged usury.

Yet this clause has been seized upon by avaricious Jews as permission to exact usury of all the nations not of Hebrew blood, ignoring the fact that when given it was limited to those peoples under the curse of God for their iniquities. It can not justly be made to mean that the Hebrews have a right to treat other nations with less righteousness than they treat their own people.

It is an unwarranted broadening to make it a permission to exact usury from all the human race except from Hebrews.

It was chiefly the acting upon this false interpretation, classing all Gentiles with these strangers, accursed of God, that had no rights they were permitted to respect, that set every Gentile Christian's hand against the Jews for fifteen hundred years.

Nothing more clearly marked the line between Christian and Hebrew during fifteen centuries than this one thing, that the Hebrews exacted usury or interest of the Gentiles while the Christians were unanimous in its denunciation, and forbade its practice.

Gentile Christian apologists for the taking of usury or interest, to overcome the force of this prohibition, are compelled to grant that Christians may be less brotherly than Hebrews: that the borrowers whether Christian or not are "strangers" to those who make them loans upon increase.

CHAPTER IV

DAVID AND SOLOMON

Devout Hebrews during the period of the Judges obeyed the Mosaic prohibition of usury or interest. It was also recognized as binding and obeyed during the reigns of David and Solomon. This was a greatly prosperous period when commerce flourished and trade was extended to the ends of the earth.

David was weak before certain temptations and his falls were grievous, but his repentance was deep and his returns to God were sincere. He never failed to regard God as supreme over him and the bestower of all his blessings. He is called the man after God's own heart, and it is also said that his heart was perfect before God. His spirit of devout worship has never been surpassed. His Psalms, in all the ages, have been accepted as expressing the true yearning after righteousness and a longing for closer communion with God.

David, in the fifteenth Psalm, expresses the thought of the earnest and reverent worshippers of his time. This Psalm declares the necessity of moral purity in those who would be citizens of Zion and dwellers in the holy hill.

"Lord, who shall abide in thy tabernacle? Who shall dwell in thy holy hill? He that walketh uprightly, and worketh righteousness, and speaketh the truth in his heart. He that backbiteth not with his tongue, nor doeth evil to his neighbor, nor taketh up a reproach against his neighbor. In whose eyes a vile person is condemned; but he honoreth them that fear the Lord. He that sweareth to his own hurt and changeth not. He that putteth not out his money to usury, nor taketh reward against the innocent. He that doeth these things shall never be moved."

The description, "He that putteth not out his money to usury," is direct and unqualified. There could be no mistaking its meaning. Those who were guilty could not claim to be citizens of Zion. There is no qualifying clause behind which the usurer could take refuge and escape condemnation.

This Psalm, prepared by the king, was chanted in the great congregation, and was a prick to the consciences of the sinners and a public reproof of all the sins mentioned. He that putteth out his money to increase received thus a public reproof in the great worshipping assembly.

Solomon, endowed with unequaled wisdom and able so clearly to discern the right, places among his proverbs a direct denunciation of this sin.

Prov. 28:8: "He that by usury and unjust gain increaseth his substance, he shall gather it for him that will pity the poor."

In this proverb the gain of usury is classed with unjust gain that shall not bless the gatherer. This is in entire harmony with other proverbs in which those who practice injustice and oppression are declared to be wanting in true wisdom and receive no benefit themselves.

"The righteousness of the upright shall deliver them: but transgressors shall be taken in their own naughtiness."

"As righteousness tendeth to life; so he that pursueth evil pursueth it to his own death."

"Whoso causeth the righteous to go astray in an evil way, he shall fall himself into his own pit; but the upright shall have good things in possession."

"Rob not the poor, because he is poor: neither oppress the afflicted in the gate: for the Lord will plead their cause, and spoil the soul of those that spoiled them."

Usury and unjust gain are joined by Solomon as sins of the same nature. It is also implied that they are necessarily connected with want of sympathy and helpfulness toward the poor. They are presented as an oppression that shall not bless the oppressor.

This proverb does not confine the evil to the borrower like the proverb, "The borrower is servant to the lender." The wrong is not confined to those of the poor to whom loans may be made. The oppression of usury is upon all the poor though they are not borrowers. They are the ultimate sufferers though the loan may be made by one rich man to another to enable him to engage in some business for profit. Usury is so bound up with injustice that its practice cannot fail to result in increasing the hard conditions of all the poor.

Solomon's reign was brilliant, and the ships of his commerce entered every port in the known world, yet usury was not necessary and was not practiced in that prosperous age.

CHAPTER V

DENUNCIATION OF JEREMIAH AND EZEKIEL

The Hebrew nation reached its summit of power and glory during the reign of King Solomon, but corruption crept in and disintegration followed, and a series of conflicts between portions of the kingdom. The laws given by Moses were neglected, and a long period of gross sinning followed. They were warned by the faithful yet hopeful prophet Isaiah that the overthrow of their nation was certain, and that their people would be carried captive to a strange land unless they forsook utterly their sins and turned to righteousness. They did not heed and the predicted calamities came upon them.

In the midst of these calamities the contemporary prophets Jeremiah and Ezekiel ministered. They differed greatly in their dispositions.

Jeremiah was a complainer. Always bemoaning his own and his people's hard lot. The Lamentations are recognized as the best extant expression of unmitigated grief. He lamented his birth because he was treated as a usurer and oppressor, when he had never exacted usury, nor had business with usurers. Jer. 15:10: "Woe, is me, my brother, that thou hast borne me a man of strife and a man of contention to the whole earth. I have neither lent on usury, nor have men lent to me on usury; yet every one of them doth curse me."

Ezekiel was always patient, faithfully proclaiming his messages, and suffering in silence. The completeness of his self-control and patient suffering is shown in the short but pathetic description of the death of his beloved wife, yet at the divine command he repressed his grief and delivered his message the following morning. Ezekiel 24:15-18: "Also the word of the Lord came unto me, saying, Son of man, behold, I take away from thee the desire of thine eyes with a stroke; yet neither shalt thou mourn nor weep, neither shall thy tears run down. Forbear to cry, make no mourning for the dead, bind the tire of thy head upon thee, and put on thy shoes upon thy feet, and cover up thy lips, and eat not the bread of men. So I spake of people in the morning; and at even my wife died; and I did in the morning as I was commanded."

These prophets were familiar with the same scenes. They met the same sins. Some have thought they exchanged messages, sending them respectively to Jerusalem and Chaldea for encouragement and confirmation. This was the opinion of Jerome.

In a catalogue of the sins prevailing in Jerusalem, for which the judgment of God came upon them, this prophet places "Usury and increase." Ezekiel 22: 7-12: "In thee have they set light by father and mother: in the midst of thee have they dealt by oppression with the stranger: in thee have they vexed the fatherless and the widow. Thou hast despised mine holy things, and hast profaned my Sabbaths. In thee are men that carry tales to shed blood: and in thee they eat upon the mountains: in the midst of thee they commit lewdness. In thee have they discovered their father's nakedness: in thee have they humbled her that was set apart for pollution. And one hath committed abomination with his neighbor's wife; and another hath lewdly defiled his daughter-in-law; and another in thee hath humbled his sister, his father's daughter. In thee have they taken gifts to shed blood; thou hast taken usury and increase, and thou hast greedily gained of thy neighbors by extortion, and hast forgotten me, saith the Lord God."

It would not be easy to give a list of more gross and flagrant sins than those associated with usury in this passage. They are all, always and everywhere, sinful. In no condition can they be lawful and right.

One of the answers familiar to both Jeremiah and Ezekiel when the people were reproved for their sins and exhorted to forsake them, that the divine judgments might be removed, was this, that their sufferings were not on their own account, but for the sins of their fathers. They thus met the charge of personal sins and claimed their sufferings were inherited and unavoidable. Their fathers had indulged in sin and they must reap the consequences. They complained that this was hardness in God. They expressed this murmur by a proverb. Jer. 31:29: "The fathers have eaten a sour grape, and the children's teeth are set on edge."

The answer of the prophet Jeremiah briefly is, that every one shall answer for his own sin. Jer. 31:30: "But every one shall die for his own iniquity: every man that eateth the sour grape, his teeth shall be set on edge."

This same proverb was repeatedly given to Ezekiel, as an excuse for continuing in sins, even when the judgments of God were upon them. The word of the Lord came more fully and explicitly to him.

Ezekiel declares that the sins of the fathers were visited on the children only when they continued in their father's iniquity. That those who forsook the sins of their fathers and were righteous, were free from the punishment of the unrighteous parents.

Ezekiel 18:1-17: "The word of God came unto me again, saying, What mean ye, that ye use this proverb concerning the land of Israel, saying, The fathers have eaten sour grapes and the children's teeth are set on edge.

As I live, saith the Lord God, ye shall not have occasion to use this proverb in Israel. Behold, all souls are mine; as the soul of the father, so also the soul of the son is mine: the soul that sinneth, it shall die. But if a man be just, and do that which is lawful and right, and hath not eaten upon the mountains, neither hath lifted up his eyes to the idols of the house of Israel, neither hath defiled his neighbor's wife, neither hath come near to a menstruous woman, (*i.e.* neither hath committed a rape,) and hath not oppressed any, but hath restored to the debtor his pledge, hath spoiled none by violence, hath given his bread to the hungry, and hath covered the naked with a garment. He that hath not given forth upon usury, neither hath taken any increase, that hath withdrawn his hand from iniquity, hath executed true judgment between man and man. Hath walked in my statutes, and hath kept my judgments, to deal truly; he is just, he shall surely live, saith the Lord God."

"If he beget a son that is a robber, a shedder of blood, and that doeth the like to any one of these things; and that doeth not any of those duties but even hath eaten upon the mountains, and defiled his neighbor's wife, hath oppressed the poor and needy, hath spoiled by violence, hath not restored the pledge, and hath lifted his eyes to the idols, hath committed abomination, hath given forth upon usury, and hath taken increase: Shall he then live? He shall not live: he hath done all these abominations; he shall surely die; his blood shall be upon him. Now, lo, if he beget a son, that seeth all his father's sins which he hath done, and considereth, and doeth not such like: that hath not eaten upon the mountains, neither hath lifted up his eyes to the idols of the house of Israel, hath not defiled his neighbor's wife, neither hath oppressed any, hath not withholden the pledge, neither hath spoiled by violence, but hath given his bread to the hungry, and hath covered the naked with a garment, that hath taken off his hand from the poor, that hath not received usury or increase, hath executed my judgments, hath walked in my statutes; he shall not die for the iniquity of his father, he shall surely live."

It will be noticed that usury or increase is here mentioned among the grossest and foulest sins of which that people were guilty. They are placed by the prophet in the worst possible company. He classifies them among those things that can never be right. There is no qualification of "increase" great or small, nor of "usury" whether the loan be domestic or commercial, whether for personal need, or to go into business, whether the borrower be poor or rich.

Usury is mentioned as *"malum per se."* "Usury and increase" are treated as sinful in themselves, just as fraud, violence, impurity, and idolatry are sinful, and can never be innocent unless their very natures are reversed. When there is fraud without dishonesty, and violence without injury, and adultery without impurity, and idolatry without false worship, then may there be "usury and increase" without injustice and oppression. "Some sins in themselves and by reason of several aggravations are more heinous in the sight of God than others," the prophet Ezekiel places "usury or increase" in the list of "abominations."

CHAPTER VI

FINANCIAL REFORM BY NEHEMIAH[1]

After seventy years of captivity of the Hebrews in Chaldea an edict was issued by Cyrus the king permitting their return to Judea. The most earnest and devout had been restless and homesick in the strange land. The restoration was led by Zerubbabel who accompanied by about five thousand of the most devout men from the various families, made their way over the long return to their former home. This was only about one-sixth of the captive population. Many preferred to remain in the land they had now adopted, and where some had been prospered, and some were perhaps less fervent in their religious zeal. This fraction of the people, however, determined to re-erect their temple and to cultivate the fields again that were given to their fathers and to rebuild the nation, the tradition of whose glory never failed to stir their hearts.

Eighty years later another company under the priest and scholar, Ezra, authorized by Artaxerxes, joined the first colony that had returned to re-occupy their own land.

---

[1] References: Ezra, Nehemiah, Bible Dictionaries.

A few years later another company was led by the patriot, Nehemiah. Nehemiah was in an honorable and lucrative position in the first court upon earth, yet he grieved over the misfortunes of his own people, and especially over the reported distress of the returned exiles. He sought leave of absence and a commission to return and co-work with his brethren for their complete re-establishment at Jerusalem.

The leave of absence was cheerfully granted and a broad commission given to take with him any who wished to return. The revenues of the king were placed at his disposal and the governors of the provinces were ordered to assist and further his work. A large company of the earnest and devout returned with him, confident of his protection and in sympathy with his mission. He deliberately reviewed the work to be done, made careful plans and was greatly successful.

The people were obedient. They cheerfully endured the privations and dangers in their devotion to their country, and in the hope of retrieving the fortunes of their depressed people.

Enemies appeared, who threatened to estop their work, but some worked while others watched, with arms in hand, ready to defend. Some wrought with one hand and held a weapon for ready defence in the other. Nehemiah and his aides, and many of the people, did not take off their clothes, but were on duty constantly—so devoted were they to the cause in which they were engaged, regaining their homes and re-establishing the worship of their fathers and rebuilding the nation.

But there was a strange interruption in this patriotic work. A sordid covetousness possessed their nobles and rulers. While the people were absorbed in their patriotic service, these persons were planning successfully to despoil them.

A cry of distress came to the ears of Nehemiah. The people found, now that they had made the sacrifice and suffered deprivations and cheerfully given their labors for the common good, they were deprived of their blessings and enslaved.

This enslavement was not to foreign rulers, but to those of their own blood. A division had grown up among their own kindred. Some had grown rich and become their masters. Others were in hopeless poverty. The distinctions came gradually or grew up among them, possibly unobserved: the rich becoming richer and the poor poorer, until the nobles held their lands and were selling their sons and daughters as chattels.

This condition was hopeless, after all their struggles for nearly a hundred years to re-establish their institutions. Neither they nor their children could, under those conditions, enjoy the fruit of all their efforts. This was no fault of theirs. There had been times of dearth and harvest failure, when some with large families were in need. The king's tribute, too, was heavy upon them and some were not able to pay and they were compelled to borrow, but had to give mortgages upon their land as security. Now lands, homes and all, had passed to the creditors and they were despondent and helpless.

This cry caused Nehemiah great distress, but Nehemiah was not like Ezra, a devout and learned priest, but without executive power, who in a like position gave way to unmitigated grief. Nehemiah was equally patriotic and conscientious, but he was also a strong leader and an independent commander. He did not call together the nobles and rulers charged with oppression and ask them what he should do. He had none of their counsel. He took counsel with himself, his own conscience, his own judgment, and worked out an independent, individual policy which he should pursue.

His sympathy was with the suffering people, and he determined to espouse their cause and to correct their wrongs. He then called the nobles and rulers and charged them to their face with oppression. He laid "the ax at the root of the tree" and charged the fault to their covetousness, to the exacting of usury or interest. It was this, he declared, that had brought them to wealth, but driven others to poverty. He demanded reparation. When they were slow to yield, he called a convocation of the people and aroused them to a due sense of the wrong they had been enduring, and laid bare the sins of the rulers and nobles. He showed the oppression by comparing their sordid and greedy conduct with the unselfish, self-sacrifice of himself and others for the common good. While he and the patriotic people were busy with hand and brain in rebuilding the nation and fighting the enemies, these usurers were busy getting in their work of ruin, gathering the property into their own hands and enslaving the patriots.

The usurers were not able to withstand this onslaught of the chief commander and the aroused people, and they made no reply. Their conduct had so evidently been contrary both to the letter and spirit of their own law, they were compelled to yield and to say meekly, "We will do as you have said."

Then he stated the terms and conditions of the reform he would institute.

1. They must return the pledges they had taken for debts, without reserve. The people must not be deprived of their land, tools, or instruments of production. The foreclosure of mortgages must be set aside and the people again given possession of their lands.

2. Interest must be returned or credited upon the debts. If the interest equaled the debt, then the debt was fully discharged. If more than the principal had been paid, then it must be returned in money or in the product of lands taken in foreclosure, the wine or oil or fruits and grains must be returned. Thus only could the wrongs be corrected and righteous adjustment be made.

There then followed a general restoration of pledges and a cancelling of debts that had been paid once in interest, and a repaying of any surplus.

3. They must take a solemn vow that this sin shall henceforth be unknown among them. The law against usury or interest must henceforth be carefully obeyed. These distinctions that had grown up among them must disappear forever, and the cause of the poverty of the many and the wealth of the few must be shunned.

To these conditions the usurers assented, made ashamed by the conduct of the noble patriot in contrast with their own selfishness, though they had not yielded until awed and compelled by the indignation of the people, which Nehemiah had enkindled against them.

This positive enforcement of the law against the taking of increase on any loan, makes unmistakably clear the interpretation of the law by the devout, earnest, sincere, God-fearing Hebrews, down to the close of the Old Testament Canon.

CHAPTER VII

TEACHINGS OF THE MASTER

Psalmist and prophets had sung of the exalted character of the coming Messiah. "Thou art fairer than the children of men: grace is poured into thy lips." "And his name shall be called Wonderful, Counselor, The Mighty God, The Everlasting Father, The Prince of Peace."

At his coming he lifted to a higher plane, by his precepts and example, the ideal of a true, noble and worthy human life. By his teachings and by his life of utter unselfishness he revealed clearly the exalted character and conduct that conformed to the Divine will.

1. Our Lord's character forbids that we should think of him for a moment as devoted to the gathering of worldly wealth. He came to minister unto, not to serve himself. Self-seeking was foreign to his nature. A great truth was spoken by the scoffers. "He saved others, himself he cannot save."

He who strives to follow in his footsteps cannot serve himself.

The whole drift of a great unselfish Christ-like soul must be for others. The whole current of his thought and effort during his life must be, to be helpful to others. Studying and striving to help others, he cannot seek wealth. "Ye cannot serve God and mammon."

It is out of harmony with the whole life and all the teachings of the Master that he should encourage or permit a means of increasing wealth forbidden by the laws given by Moses and classed among the vilest of sins by the prophets.

2. Again: He did not undo the teachings of the prophets, but enlarged their scope. He showed by word and example how the true spirit of the teachings of the old dispensation led to self-sacrifice for the welfare of others. Matt. 5:17: "Think not that I am come to destroy the law, or the prophets: I am not come to destroy but to fulfill."

Fulfill, here, is more than to obey. It is in antithesis with destroy, and means to perfect and complete.

The old ceremonial forms of religious worship, pointed to the advent of one who should be a perfect sacrifice for sin, typified by the daily sacrifice of bulls and rams. The sacrifice typified, was completed in Him.

The moral enactments were not set aside, but they were given a completed meaning; that is they were made to reach beyond the external to the hidden desires and affections of the heart. He taught that mere external compliance was not sufficient in the All Seeing Eye. The affections and desires of the soul must be in agreement.

Thus we have the explanation of the law of chastity, completed, requiring purity of the soul. So murder is not merely the external act, but the law for murder, completed, forbids enmity or hatred hidden in the heart.

The requirements for mutual helpfulness were also perfected or completed.

The old law required the helping of a brother in need.

Deut. 15:7, 8: "If there be among you a poor man of one of thy brethren within any of thy gates in the land which the Lord thy God giveth thee, thou shalt not harden thy heart, nor shut thine hand from thy poor brother. But thou shalt open thine hand wide unto him, and shalt surely lend him sufficient for his need, in that which he wanteth."

This was completed so as to extend the help to all sufferers, though not kindred nor friendly, and though they may not be able nor willing to repay. Luke 6:35: "But love ye your enemies, and do good, and lend, hoping for nothing again; and your reward shall be great, and ye shall be the children of the Highest: for he is kind unto the unthankful, and to the evil."

The old law permitted the lender to take a pledge to secure the return of "as much again," that is, the loan without interest. The Master enjoins being helpful though the principal should never be repaid. To take a pledge or mortgage and add the interest would greatly harden the conditions for the borrower. It would be a step backward and not forward in the way of helpfulness to others.

Again, the year of Jubilee was a kind of legal time limit to debts. All obligations were then cancelled. No debt could be collected. The selfish Hebrew feared to make a loan shortly before Jubilee lest it should not be repaid promptly and his claim would become worthless. Deut. 15:9: "Beware that there be no thought in thy wicked heart, saying, The seventh year, the year of release is at hand; and thine eye be evil toward thy poor brother, and thou givest him naught; and he cry unto the Lord against thee and it be sin unto thee." In his heart the old Hebrew might have a desire to press his claim but the law protected the debtor. This law for the release of the debtor from the payment of principal without interest is completed so as to require sincere and hearty forgiveness.

Our Lord taught his disciples to ask for forgiveness of God only as they forgave their debtors, Matt. 6:12: "And forgive us our debts, as we forgive our debtors." The commercial terms here used show this to be the completion of the law as touching the creditor and his released debtor.

3. Again, he broke down the artificial barriers, the distinction of Hebrew and Gentile, Greek and Barbarian, bond and free.

The love and sympathy and helpfulness among men was no longer to be limited to such narrow bounds, but must be wide as the race. "Who is my neighbor?" is so answered that every man must be neighbor to every other man, and the object of his care and help. All are of one blood, and all God's children. He gave one law for all classes and conditions in all times. He so expounded the old commandments and so condensed them, that they became the one law of love. Whosoever is governed by supreme love to God, and loves his neighbor as himself, has fulfilled the law. He would thus bind all men together, and all to the throne of God, by the one bond of love.

But he further intensified the obligations of love, by his own special command. John 15:12: "This is my commandment, that ye love one another, as I have loved you." And he adds it to the decalogue, John 13:34: "A new commandment I give unto you, that ye love one another as I have loved you that ye also love one another." This new command requires that men shall love their brethren above themselves and be ready to sacrifice for their welfare. As he gave his life, so also he commanded that men should sacrifice for their fellows.

Those who hear his voice and have the spirit of obedience go to the ends of the earth, and make any sacrifice that may be required for the uplifting of fallen men.

The law forbidding the Hebrews exacting usury of their brethren, of the stranger who had accepted their faith and kept the passover, of the stranger, sojourner who dwelt among them, of everybody except the Canaanite who was under the condemnation of God, could not have been annulled or suspended by the divine Master who thus draws together and embraces as one family the whole race. The ties of Christian brotherhood are not less strong than the ties of Hebrew blood. The converts from heathen to Christian faith are not less dear to the missionary than the proselytes to the Hebrew faith were to the Pharisees. The foreigner who comes into a Christian community must not be treated with less justice and kindness than the wandering Arab who strolled into Jerusalem for a trade. It cannot be that the relation between Christians is like that between the Hebrew and the criminal Canaanites who were convicted of capital crimes and under sentence of death. As usury was repugnant to that spirit of justice and brotherly love that obtained in the Hebrew State, much more is it repugnant to that closer brotherhood into which we are drawn by the divine Lord.

4. Again, He was a friend of the poor and lowly. This was foretold by the song of the virgin, when assured that she should be the mother of the Savior. Luke 51:52, 53: "He hath put down the mighty from their seats, and exalted them of low degree. He hath filled the hungry with good things; and the rich He hath sent empty away."

The prophets foretold that He should be the friend of the poor. He pointed John to the fulfilment of these prophecies in proof of his Messiahship.

In his first address in the explanation of the new dispensation he began by saying, "Blessed are the poor in spirit." The literal rendering would be, "Blessed are the poor, to the Spirit." This is the dative singular with the definite article. He is speaking of external conditions as contrasted with spiritual blessings, and those conditions thought wretched in the world were especially favorable for the development of grace. The poor, humble, mourning, suffering, and persecuted were especially blessed in his kingdom.

The word rendered poor does not mean pauper. There is a great difference. The poor may be industrious, self-reliant and self-supporting. There is no hint of dependence.

In Luke he says, "Blessed are ye poor." When at the rich man's table, he told his host that he would be more blessed if he should make the next feast to the poor and defective, that could make him no return.

He was uncompromising in his denunciation of the rich. Luke 6:24: "But woe unto you that are rich, for ye have received your consolation." He showed the danger of riches in the parable of the sower. Matt. 13:22: "He also that received seed among thorns is he that heareth the word; and the care of this world, and the deceitfulness of riches choke the word, and it becometh unfruitful."

Where grace is to be cultivated and flourish, the "greed of gain" must not enter. The young man who came to him, whom he loved for his sweet disposition and excellent character, he turned away by the answer that his wealth was incompatible with his salvation. He must part from his riches. When the disciples were surprised, he made it more emphatic, Matt. 19:24: "And again I say unto you, it is easier for a camel to go through the eye of a needle, than for a rich man to enter the kingdom of God." And when they felt that this made salvation impossible, he declared it could only be possible by the exercise of omnipotent, divine grace.

Zaccheus, the one rich man whose conversion is recorded, surrendered his ill-gotten gain fourfold and gave away half of the remainder before salvation came to his house. The temptation to trust and lean upon riches is irresistible.

Our Lord did not make wealth more dangerous than under the Mosaic dispensation by removing the restraint that was there put upon it. As a friend to the poor he did not give wealth an advantage it did not have before.

5. The whole drift of his teachings limited and restrained accumulation of wealth. The parable of the rich fool is a forcible presentation of its human folly on the earthly side.

"Whose shall these things be?"

"Lay not up for yourselves treasures upon earth, where moth and rust doth corrupt, and where thieves break through and steal: But lay up for yourselves treasures in heaven, where neither moth nor rust doth corrupt, and where thieves do not break through and steal: For where your treasure is, there will your heart be also."

The result is irresistible; when engaged in storing earthly treasure, the heart will be earthly; or if laying up treasures in heaven, the heart will reach heavenward. He who labors for a heavenly reward, will be heavenly minded.

Treasures are stored for eternity, when used for the bringing out of that which shall survive the grave; for the bringing out the highest divine type of manhood and womanhood, in ourselves, in our children, and in all the children of men.

Treasures expended in the development of immortals shall be found when the earthly and temporal scenes have passed away. That which is expended in the uplifting of the race shall be our eternal reward.

Giving, giving, not hoarding is commended. Productive industry he enforced by his example, the carpenter that wrought for his daily bread. He chose workmen to be his followers. He taught economy in the command to take up the fragments of the food miraculously created "that nothing be lost," yet unreserved giving was the lesson he inculcated and illustrated in his life. To follow his example, we must produce and produce much, yet what we gain is to be expended, so as to promote the highest welfare of all mankind. We must not store the fruits of our labor, but expend, not as a spendthrift who wastes, but judiciously and wisely for God and man. Our giving is only limited by the ability and facility to produce. Our Lord did not greatly add to the temptation to hoard by delivering the earthly treasures from the decay by "moth and rust" and instead permitting their increase. Our hoarding of earthly treasures must be limited, because of our disposition to trust in them. We must always be so dependent that we shall pray truly with the spirit of dependence, "Give us this day our daily bread." "Give me neither poverty nor riches; feed me with food convenient for me."

Thrift does not require that we shall hoard an amount that will support us through life, much less that we shall lay up a fortune, that shall free our children from the necessity of productive labor. The spirit of the Master's teachings is, that each age shall produce and spend its product for its own advancement, then each succeeding age shall be better fitted to produce and care for itself and so advance the coming generations. "Go work today in my vineyard." Now is the time to give and do for the generation yet unborn.

CHAPTER VIII

PARABLES OF THE TALENTS AND THE POUNDS

Our Lord mentions usury by name only in the parables of the talents and pounds. Matt. 25:14-30; Luke 19:12-27. Usury is mentioned in these passages incidentally to meet the excuses of worthless servants, but in both as the unjust and oppressive act of a hard and dishonest man. These references to usury are in entire harmony with the expressions of David and Solomon, and of Jeremiah and Ezekiel.

These servants in the parables were slaves, who owed their service to their master and for whom he was responsible.

The lesson in both parables is the necessity of faithfulness. The faithful servants are rewarded and the unfaithful punished in both. Yet there is a special lesson in each.

The parable of the talents shows that an equal reward shall be given all who are equally faithful, though the means and opportunities afforded one may far exceed those granted another. One was given five talents and another but two; one gained five and the other two, yet both equally faithful, are directed to enter into the joy of their lord.

The unfaithful servant brings his talent with an excuse, which is a charge against the character of his master, "I knew thee that thou art an hard man reaping where thou hast not sown, and gathering where thou hast not strewed," "so there thou hast which is thine."

The master in reply showed the inconsistency of the excuse by assuming that he bore the hard character charged upon him by his slave, "Thou wicked and slothful servant, thou knewest that I reap where I sowed not, and gather where I have not strewed: Thou oughtest therefore to have put my money to the exchangers, and then at my coming I should have received mine own with usury." It is "interest" in the Revised Version.

This interview may be paraphrased as follows:

The unfaithful servant said: "I know the kind of a man you are. You are dishonest. You take what does not belong to you. You reap what other people sow, and you take up what others earn. I was afraid of you: Here is all that you gave me and all that belongs to you."

The master said: "You are merely excusing yourself. You are a lazy faithless slave. If I am the hard man you say I am, taking what does not belong to me and gathering the sowings and earnings of others, you could have met that condition without trouble to yourself, by giving my money to the usurers and then at my coming I could have received my unjust gain. Your excuse is inconsistent, you condemn yourself. You are an indolent and worthless slave. Begone to your punishment."

It is clearly implied that unearned increase, reaping and gathering without sowing, could be gained through the exchangers. If this was what was demanded, the servant could have secured this with no effort on his part. His charge against the master was a mere pretence to excuse his own want of personal faithfulness, and the master's reply was fitted to this pretense.

This is in entire harmony with the opinion our Lord expressed of the exchangers when he called them thieves and drove them out of the temple. It would be wholly inconsistent for him to advise an honest and faithful servant to place any portion of the property in their hands. His advice can only come from the standpoint of a dishonest master such as his servant called him.

The parable of the pounds shows the degrees of faithfulness in those who have equal opportunities. With the same opportunities one may far surpass another, because more faithful to his trust, his reward is proportionately greater.

In this parable each servant received the same, but the gains and rewards differ. By diligence one gained ten pounds and is commended and given authority over ten cities. Another gained five pounds. He is also commended and given authority over five cities.

Another, who had given no service, came with his pound but without increase. This was a proof of his unfaithfulness. He endeavors to shield himself like the servant with the talent, by charging injustice and oppression on his master. "I feared thee because thou art an austere man: thou takest up that thou layest not down, and reapest that thou didst not sow."

His master turned on him because his own reason was inconsistent with his conduct and a mere shield for his indolence and worthlessness. "Out of thine own mouth will I judge thee, thou wicked servant. Thou knowest that I was an austere man, taking up that I laid not down, and reaping that I did not sow. Wherefore gavest thou not my money into the bank, that at my coming I might have required mine own with usury."

This interview may also be paraphrased.

The unfaithful slave came and said: "Lord I have carefully kept all that thou gavest me. I knew that thou wast an exacting master, taking what did not belong to you and gathering what others sow."

The master says: "Now stop right there and I will judge you by your own excuse out of your own mouth. You say you knew me to be exacting and dishonest, taking more than belonged to me. Now, knowing this, why did you not serve me by giving my money to the bank, and then at my coming you could have brought me my money with my unjust gain and that would have pleased a hard man like me, without effort on your part. You are only giving this as an excuse for your own unfaithfulness. You are a wicked slave."

The master admits that he would be a hard man, if he reaped what another sowed, or took up what belonged to another, but assuming that this was his character, even this could have been met without trouble to the slave through the bank. This is a clear recognition of usury as unjust gain.

Exchangers were little more than the pawn-brokers of today and a bank was a pawn-shop where pledges were stored. The money loaned upon any pawn was much less than its full value. The increase of the loan soon made it more than the value of the pledge which was then forfeited, and the pawn was sold by the broker.

These parables are here dwelt upon, for they are so frequently misunderstood and misapplied. In a large volume on "Banking," the writer found the words of the master quoted, "Wherefore then gavest not thou my money into the bank, that at my coming I might have required my own with usury." And they were quoted as a solemn direction of the divine Master to deposit money in the bank.

To quote from these parables in the defense of usury is as flagrant a perversion of the truth as the famous quotation to prove that Paul encouraged theft. "Let him that stole, steal."

The lessons of these parables are in entire harmony with the law of Moses and the teachings of the prophets and Nehemiah. In these parables the usurer is presented as a hard man, exacting that which he has not earned and to which he has no right.

The teachings of the Master did not permit what had been forbidden in all the ages.

CALVIN ELLIOTT

CHAPTER IX

PRACTICE OF THE DISCIPLES

The conditions in the very early church were not such as to make prominent the sin of usury. Many of the disciples were very poor and from the humblest walks of life. I Cor. 1:27-28: "But God hath chosen the foolish things of the world to confound the wise; and God hath chosen the weak things of the world to confound the things that are mighty; and the base things of the world, and things which are despised, hath God chosen, yea, and the things which are not, to bring to nought things that are."

The practice of the disciples was, however, in entire harmony with the teachings of Moses and the Master, and in accord with the prohibition of usury. Later, in the time of the apostolic fathers when the church came face to face with this sin, there was but one voice and that in the denunciation, for the fathers were unanimous in its condemnation.

(1) The first disciples did not loan, but gave to their needy brethren. The early converts held their property so subject to a general call that some have thought they had a community of goods.

Acts 2:44, 45: "And all that believed were together, and had all things common; * * * and sold their possessions and goods, and parted them to all men, as every man had need."

It is evident they did not assist their brethren with "loans," but with gifts; much less did they take the opportunity to secure increase on loans.

The suffering poor were their especial care. They gave of their poverty for the relief of the suffering. Many called by the Spirit were in want, and many came to want through the severe persecutions to which they were subjected. This was especially true of the converts in Jerusalem. For these large collections were received from the churches in Macedonia and in Corinth.

They were commanded to care for the needy of their own house. I Tim. 5:8: "But if any provide not for his own, and especially for those of his own house, he hath denied the faith, and is worse than an infidel." Paul, in giving directions to Timothy, as to the care of their poor, requires aid to be given to "widows indeed," those who have no children; but those who have children or nephews are to look to them and be supported by them, and if any person refuses to care for his widowed mother or grandmother or dependent aunt, "he hath denied the faith and is worse than an infidel."

(2) They were diligent in business. They provided things honest in the sight of all men.

Paul set the example during his itinerate ministry by working at his trade to secure his support and his dictum has been accepted as both divine and human wisdom ever since. "If any will not work neither shall he eat."

Diligence was enjoined for self-support, and that others might be helped. Eph. 4:28: "Let him that stole, steal no more; but rather let him labor, working with his hands, the things which is good, that he may have to give to him that needeth." The effort was first by labor to be independent and then also to come to the relief of the feeble, the sick, the poor, and the needy. That a man could honestly secure a livelihood without productive labor was foreign to their way of thinking. If any did not work he did not deserve a living, nor was he an honest man. No one was at liberty to be idle. Productive effort must not be relaxed. There was no retiring for the enjoyment of a competency.

There was no thought of such a provision to free them from the effort for the daily bread. The surplus product was given for the aid of others, to those who had claims of kinship first, then to all who had need.

The instant a man failed to produce he began to consume. There is no hint anywhere that it entered any of their minds that they could stop production and live in ease from the increase of what they had produced and the supply grow no less; that the meal and oil should not fail, but be handed down unimpaired to their children.

(3) Covetousness was hated and denounced and classed with the most flagrant violations of the moral law.

Covetousness is an inordinate regard for wealth of any kind. This may be shown in the greed of seeking it, without proper regard for the rights of others; or in parsimony or stinginess in holding it, when there are rightful claims upon it.

James 5:1-6: "Go to now, ye rich men, weep and howl for your miseries that shall come upon you. Your riches are corrupted, and your garments are moth eaten. Your gold and silver is cankered; and the rust of them shall be witness against you, and shall eat your flesh as it were fire. You have heaped treasure together for the last days.

"Behold, the hire of the laborers who have reaped down your fields, which is of you kept back by fraud, crieth: and the cries of them which have reaped are entered into the ears of the Lord of Sabbath.

"Ye have lived in pleasure on the earth, and been wanton; ye have nourished your hearts, as in a day of slaughter. Ye have condemned and killed the just, and he doth not resist you."

Covetousness may also be shown in undue respect for wealth when in the hands of others. This is reproved in James 2:1-7. "My brethren, have not the faith of our Lord Jesus Christ, the Lord of glory, with respect of persons. For if there come unto your assembly a man with a gold ring, in goodly apparel, and there come also a poor man in vile raiment; and ye have respect to him that weareth the gay clothing, and say unto him, Sit thou here in a good place; and say to the poor man, Stand thou there, or sit here under my footstool: Are ye not then partial in yourselves, and become the judges of evil thoughts? Hearken, my beloved brethren, hath not God chosen the poor of this world rich in faith, and heirs of the kingdom which he hath promised them that love him? But ye have despised the poor. Do not rich men oppress you, and draw you before the judgment seats? Do not they blaspheme that worthy name by which ye are called?"

Covetousness was a secret sin often indulged when the outward forms of righteousness were observed. Usurers were the open representatives of flagrant covetousness in all the ages. Usury was not named among them as becometh saints.

(4) The early disciples kept out of debt. The early Christians were not borrowers. In both dispensations borrowing was only resorted to in hard necessity. The borrower was second to the beggar. The borrowing was but for a short time, and the loan was returned as soon as absolute wants were supplied.

The doctrine and practice of the early church was to owe no man anything. Rom. 13:8: "Owe no man anything, but to love one another: for he that loveth another hath fulfilled the law."

Indebtedness was to be avoided as compromising the faith in the eyes of others and detrimental to the development of grace in the disciples.

This was the direct command of Paul. This commandment required the payment of all honest obligations. The Christian then as now who failed to acknowledge his obligations and meet them in full as he was able was wanting in the spirit of righteousness and unfaithful to his own convictions of right and duty.

The payment of a debt was the return in full of the loan received.

Any Christian conscience at that time would have been satisfied with the settlement approved and commanded by Nehemiah. The debt was fully discharged when payments equaled the loan by whatever name those payments were called.

This text also required that they keep out of debt. By no distortion of the text can it be made to mean less. Chalmers on this passage comments as follows: "But though to press the duty of our text in the extreme and rigorous sense of it—yet I would fain aspire towards the full and practical establishment of it, so that the habit might become at length universal, not only paying all debts, but even by making conscience never to contract, and therefore never to owe any. For although this might never be reached, it is well it should be looked at, nay moved forward to, as a sort of optimism, every approximation to which were a distinct step in advance, both for the moral and economic good of society. For, first, in the world of trade, one can not be insensible to the dire mischief that ensues from the spirit often so rampant, of an excessive and unwarrantable speculation—so as to make it the most desirable of all consummations that the system of credit should at length give way, and what has been termed the ready-money system, the system of immediate payments in every commercial transaction, should be substituted in its place. The adventurer who, in the walks of merchandise, trades beyond his means is often actuated by a passion as intense, and we fear too, as criminal, as is the gamester, who in the haunts of fashionable dissipation, stakes beyond his fortune. But it is not the injury alone, which the ambition that precipitates him into such deep and desperate hazards, brings upon his own character, neither is it the ruin that the splendid bankruptcy in which it terminates brings upon his own family.

These are not the only evils which we deprecate—for over and above these there is a far heavier disaster, a consequence in the train of such proceedings, of greatly wider and more malignant operation still, on the habit and condition of the working classes, gathered in hundreds around the mushroom establishment, and then thrown adrift among the other wrecks of its overthrow, in utter helplessness and destitution on society. This frenzy of men hasting to be rich, like fever in the body natural, is a truly sore distemper in the body politic. No doubt they are also sufferers themselves, piercing their own hearts through with many sorrows; but it is the contemplation of this suffering in masses, which the sons and daughters of industry in humble life so often earn at their hands, that has ever led me to rank them among the chief pests and disturbers of a commonwealth."

To this may be added an extract from "Short Instructions for Early Masses by the Paulist Fathers." "The fact of the matter is, dear brethren, that there is too much laxity of conscience among our people on this question of contracting debts, of borrowing money, of running up bills with little or no hope of ever paying them. We have all of us no doubt come across people who consider themselves quite religious who owe money to their neighbors for years, and never make an effort to pay what they owe or even to offer an excuse for their negligence in such important matters.

There are some professional debtors who think the world owes them a living, and who spend a good part of their time figuring out how much they can get out of the land and from those who dwell thereon. To have to pay rent is their greatest grievance, and after being trusted for a few months, they find it much cheaper to move to other quarters than to pay what they owe.

Then there are others who must dress extravagantly, no matter what it costs, and in consequence have nothing left to pay for the things they eat or drink. Do they on this account deny themselves any of the good things of this life? Not at all; on the contrary, every business man will tell you the same story—these people want the best and are the most exacting in their demands.

Now, I repeat, there is too much laxity about contracting debts and too little conscience about the necessity of paying for what we use. St. Paul's warning should ring in the ears of every debtor: "Owe no man anything." It will not do for such people to come to confession and say they contracted debts and are not able to pay what they owe. Confession will not relieve them of their obligation, and they must begin at once and make an effort to lessen the debts they owe in the past and learn a lesson in economy and strive against contracting new burdens. This will help us to clear off the old ones.

It is not edifying, nor is it conducive to good fellowship, nor does it help to make our religion better known and better loved, to find people, dressed in the finest, coming Sunday after Sunday to mass while they are heavily in debt to their grocer or butcher or landlord, who may be in the very same pew with them. This is certain, it convinces such men in business that the debtor's religion is not very sincere.

In a word, brethren, it is far better to live in less pretentious dwellings, dress more soberly and eat more sparingly than to owe any man anything. Pay what thou owest, and then you may walk honestly among all men."

Freedom from debt is necessary to the independence of the man who does right and answers only to God. Struggle as he may the man is not free who is under obligations to others. He is hindered in his conduct; he is not always conscious of it, but nevertheless there is a real binding or fettering of his actions. It influences his gifts, for what he holds is not his own and the owner may criticize his benevolence.

An easy conscience and sound sleep is the portion of the man who is under no obligations to another. He looks the whole world in the face, who owes no man a cent.

He is free from distracting business relations with his brethren and brotherly love may abound. The exhortation of Paul is in connection with brotherly love, and of all external relations, debt hinders the free flow of sympathy among brethren.

The early disciples endeavored to avoid all debt. Much less did they pay a premium for the privilege. They only borrowed in hard necessity; but borrowing on usury to make a profit by it was as repellant to the Christian conscience then as complicity with theft or fraud. It marked a man as anxious to share in unrighteous gain. His own conscience placed him among those who are discontented with their lawful estate and guilty of that covetousness which is idolatry. I Tim. 6:6-11: "But godliness with contentment is great gain. For we brought nothing into this world, and it is certain we can carry nothing out. And having food and raiment, let us be therewith content. But they that will be rich fall into temptation and a snare, and into many foolish and hurtful lusts, which drown men in destruction and perdition. For the love of money is the root of all evil: which while some coveted after, they have erred in the faith, and pierced themselves through with many sorrows. But thou, O man of God, flee these things; and follow after righteousness, godliness, faith, love, patience, meekness."

CHAPTER X

CHURCH HISTORY

The Church, from the time of the apostles, was emphatic in its denunciation of usury.

Schaff-Herzog says: "All the apostolic fathers condemned the taking of usury." The Encyclopedia of Religious Knowledge declares the same.

Chrysostom said: "Nothing is baser in this world than usury, nothing more cruel."

Basil describes a scene so real that we can scarcely realize that he wrote over fifteen hundred years ago. After stating the usurer's protestations of having no money, to the victim, who seeks a loan without interest, he says: "Then the suppliant mentions interest and utters the word security. All is changed. The frown is relaxed; with a genial smile he recounts old family connections. Now it is 'My friend, I will see if I have any money by me. Yes, there is that very sum which a man, I know, has left in my hands in deposit for profit. He named a very heavy interest. However, I will certainly take something off and give it to you on better terms.' With pretenses like this he fawns on the wretched victim and induces him to swallow the barb."

Of the man who has borrowed on interest, he says: "At first he is bright and joyous and shines with another's splendor * * * now night brings no rest, no sun is bright. He hates the days that are hurrying on, for time as it runs adds the interest to its tale."

The fathers unanimously condemned the taking of interest, Tertullian, Cyprian, Ambrose, Augustine and Jerome can be quoted against it. The popes followed the teachings of the fathers and forbade it under severe penalties. The priests guilty of this sin were degraded from their orders. The laymen found guilty were excommunicated. Interest paid could be reclaimed, not only from the usurer but from his heirs. A bargain, though confirmed by an oath never to claim back the interest paid, was declared not binding. This action of the popes was confirmed by councils.

Charlemagne, in France, forbid the taking of usury either by priests or laity.

A council at Westminster (1126) approved the degradation of all clergy, who were guilty of this practice.

Archbishop Sands said: "This canker (usury) hath corrupted all England."

A council in Vienna (1311) reaffirmed the denunciations of previous popes and councils, and then adds: "If any shall obstinately persist in the error of presuming to affirm that the taking of usury is not a sin, we decree that he shall be punished as a heretic."

There is no record of the repeal of any of these edicts.

The leaders of the Protestant reformation also denounced usury.

Luther was violent in his opposition, using the strongest language he could command. "Whoever eats up, robs and steals the nourishment of another, commits as great a murder, as he who carves a man or utterly undoes him. Such does a usurer, and he sits the while on his stool, when he ought rather to be hanging from the gallows."

Melancthon, Beza and others are accounted against usury.

The decisions of Ecclesiastical Councils were numerous and emphatic until the seventeenth century. Since that time interest taking has become common, all but universal, but there is no record found anywhere of its direct approval by any ecclesiastical body. The Church has come to tolerate it but has never given it official approval.

Usury has not been included in any creed or confession of faith, nor has it been directly approved by any council or general assembly.

The truth has not been left in any age without its witness. There have always been those more or less prominent in the Church who contended that it was unjust and oppressive. Some of them have been of world-wide distinction. The writer has a letter written him by John Clark Ridpath, the historian, expressing his agreement with the views presented in these pages. Another of these is brilliant John Ruskin, recently deceased. Quotations from him will close this review.

"I have not so perverted my soul nor palsied my brain as to expect to be advantaged by that adhesion (usury). I do not expect that because I have gathered much to find Nature or man gathering more for me; to find eighteen pence in my box in the morning instead of the shilling as a reward of my continence, or to make an income of my Koran by lending it to poor scholars. If I think he can read it and will carefully turn the leaves by the outside, he is welcome to read it for nothing."

"Thus in all other possible or conceivable cases, the moment our capital is increased by having lent it, be it but the estimation of a hair, that hair-breadth of increase is usury, just as much as stealing a farthing is theft no less than stealing a million."

CHAPTER XI

CALVIN'S LETTER ON USURY

A mere hint of encouragement to the usurer came from Calvin. In a letter, to a friend, he hesitatingly expressed opinions that have ever since been quoted in defense of the practice. He alone of all the reformers took a doubtful stand. He has often been referred to and given great credit for his opinion, even by those who utterly reject all the doctrines he most earnestly advocated. The fear that he expressed near the opening, that some word might be seized to take more license than he would allow had reason, for this letter has been the basis for all the apologies for usury that have ever been attempted. In these last days all who have tried to present fully the moral law as comprehended in the ten commandments have felt called upon to make some apology for the prevailing practice of usury in connection with the eighth command. They all refer to this letter. Sometimes there is a brief quotation, given in Latin and left untranslated, to convince the ignorant, for Calvin wrote in Latin.

Letter of Calvin: *De Usuris Responsum.*

"I have not yet essayed what could fitly be answered to the question put to me; but I have learned by the example of others with how great danger this matter is attended. For if all usury is condemned tighter fetters are imposed on the conscience than the Lord himself would wish. Or if you yield in the least, with that pretext, very many will at once seize upon unlicensed freedom, which can then be restrained by no moderation or restriction. Were I writing to you alone I would fear this the less; for I know your good sense and moderation, but as you ask counsel in the name of another, I fear, lest he may allow himself far more than I wish by seizing upon some word, yet confident that you will look closely into his character and from the matter that is here treated judge what is expedient, and to what extent, I shall open my thoughts to you.

"And first, I am certain that by no testimony of Scripture is usury wholly condemned. For the sense of that saying of Christ, 'Lend, hoping for nothing again' (Luke 6:35), has up to this time been perverted; the same as another passage when speaking of splendid feasts and the desire of the rich to be received in turn, he commands them rather to summon to these feasts, the blind, the lame, and other needy men, who lie at the cross-roads and have not the power to make a like return. Christ wished to restrain men's abuse of lending, commands them to lend to those from whom there is no hope of receiving or regaining anything; and his words ought to be interpreted, that while he would command loans to the poor without expectation of repayment or the receipt of interest, he did not mean at the same time to forbid loans to the rich with interest, any more than the injunction to invite the poor to our feasts did not imply that the mutual invitation of friends to feasts is in consequence prohibited. Again the law of Moses was political and should not influence us beyond what justice and philanthropy will bear.

"It could be wished that all usury and the name itself were first banished from the earth. But as this cannot be accomplished it should be seen what can be done for the public good. Certain passages of Scripture remain in the Prophets and Psalms in which the Holy Spirit inveighs against usury. Thus a city is described as wicked because usury is practiced in the forum and streets, but as the Hebrew word means frauds in general, this cannot be interpreted so strictly. But if we concede that the prophet there mentions usury by name, it is not a matter of wonder that among the great evils which existed, he should attack usury. For wherever gains are farmed out, there are generally added, as inseparable, cruelty, and numberless other frauds and deceits.

"On the other hand it is said in praise of a pious and holy man 'that he putteth not out his money to usury.' Indeed it is very rare for a man to be honest and yet a usurer.

"Ezekiel goes even further (Ezek. 22:12). Enumerating the crimes which inflamed the wrath of the Lord against the Jews, he uses two words, one of which means usury, and is derived from a root meaning to consume; the other word means increase or addition, doubtless because one devoted to his private gain takes or rather extorts it from the loss of his neighbor. It is clear that the prophets spake even more harshly of usury because it was forbidden by name among the Jews, and when therefore it was practiced against the express command of God, it merited even heavier censure.

"But when it is said, that as the cause of our state is the same, the same prohibition of usury should be retained, I answer that there is some difference in what pertains to the civil state. Because the surroundings of the place in which the Lord placed the Jews, as well as other circumstances, tended to this, that it might be easy for them to deal among themselves without usury, while our state today is very different in many respects. Therefore usury is not wholly forbidden among us unless it be repugnant both to Justice and to Charity.

"It is said, 'Money does not beget money.' What does the sea beget? What does a house from the letting of which I receive a rent? Is money born from roofs and walls? But on the other hand both the earth produces and something is brought from the sea which afterward produces money, and the convenience of a house can be bought and sold for money. If therefore more profit can be derived from trading through the employment of money than from the produce of a farm, the purpose of which is subsistence, should one who lets some barren farm to a farmer, receiving in return a price or part of the produce, be approved, and one who loans money to be used for profit be condemned? And when one buys a farm for money does not that farm produce other money yearly? And whence is derived the profit of the merchant? You will say from his diligence and his industry. Who doubts that idle money is wholly useless? Who asks a loan of me does not intend to keep what he receives idle by him. Therefore the profit does not arise from the money, but from the product that results from its use or employment. I therefore conclude that usury must be judged, not by a particular passage of Scripture, but simply by the rules of equity. This will be made clearer by an example. Let us imagine a rich man with large possessions in farms and rents, but with little money. Another man not so rich, nor with such large possessions as the first, but has more ready money. The latter being about to buy a farm with his own money, is asked by the wealthier for a loan. He who makes the loan may stipulate for a rent or interest for his money and further that the farm may be mortgaged to him until the principal is paid, but until it is paid, he will be content with the interest or usury on the loan. Why then shall this contract with a mortgage, but only for the profit of the money, be condemned, when a much harsher, it may be, of leasing or renting a farm at large annual rent, is approved?

"And what else is it than to treat God like a child, when we judge of objects by mere words and not from their nature, as if virtue can be distinguished from vice by a form of words.

"It is not my intention to fully examine the matter here. I wished only to show what you should consider more carefully. You should remember this, that the importance of the question lies not in the words but in the thing itself."

Those acquainted with Calvin's "Institutes" will not fail to notice the timid manner in which he treats the subject, as if uncertain of his ground and endeavoring to excuse usury to please his friend. This letter is wanting in that positive air of assured certainty that breathes inspired authority and lends a charm to his "Institutes." He is nearest himself when he bursts out, "It could be wished that all usury and the name itself were banished from the earth."

The letter is here given in full because often more force is carried by the reference to a great name than by the study of his argument. A careful reading of this letter does not reveal a positive approval of usury. He merely excuses it by suggesting other evils that he thinks worse; for instance, that land rentals may be worse than the usury of money. He does not mention the necessary oppression of the poor tenants by the loan upon a mortgage.

It is proof of the weakness of the case when this letter is the most favorable that can be presented from any ecclesiastic.

CHAPTER XII

PERMANENCY OF THE PROHIBITION

It is sometimes urged that the law of Moses with regard to usury was not intended to be permanent but was only a wise and beneficent regulation for that people in their peculiar condition; that as the ceremonial was done away by the incoming of the New Testament dispensation, so this prohibition was annulled and should be reckoned among the effete laws of the ancient Hebrews.

In answer to this contention it may be replied:

(1) This prohibition is not ceremonial. It has no connection with the rites and forms of their religion. It touches their character and conduct but has no place in their forms of worship.

(2) Nothing can be presented from the Mosaic laws to prove that this prohibition was only of a temporary character. It is in entire harmony with the spirit of helpfulness and especially the protection of the weak, that is so characteristic of the Mosaic order.

No induction from any of the Old Testament writers can be fairly made to limit its application. The prophets place usury in the catalogue of sins that are always and everywhere offensive to God. Nehemiah condemns it as destructive to personal and civic freedom.

(3) There is no hint of its discontinuance in the new dispensation. The Master gave a spiritual completeness to this law as he did to all enactments requiring external moral character. He classed the usurers, in his parables, among the dishonest, who took up what they had not laid down.

The disciples, in their poverty and persecutions, were not specially tempted by this sin, and it is not therefore prominent in their history. But there is nothing in their teachings or practice that is not in entire harmony with the binding continuance of the Mosaic prohibition, and their practice and teaching are just such as we should expect from Christian people in their condition and circumstances who recognized the prohibition as permanent.

(4) The apostolic fathers, as the church grew and came into contact with the world and was beginning to share in the business of the world, to a man, regarded the prohibition as in full force and its observance as one of the marked characteristics of the Christian, distinguishing him from the worldling and the Jew. Conditions in the apostolic age did not make this prominent but when the conditions were changed and the church came in conflict with this sin, it is clearly seen that the law was in a continuous binding force through the whole period.

The later fathers were of the opinion, unanimously, that it was in full force, not temporary or provincial, but binding for all time and upon all people. That it is suspended is a modern idea, a suggestion of the world to the church within the last few hundred years.

CHAPTER XIII

OUR CHANGED CONDITIONS

The changed conditions of the race in these last years are urged as a sufficient reason for annulling this law. It is admitted that it was righteous and beneficent in ages long past but with the new light and new conditions of the present it is effete, inapplicable and unjust. They call attention to the vast extension of commerce, to the marvelously increased facilities for travel, transportation and intercommunication; to the innumerable and wonderful inventions that in their application have brightened our civilization. They exalt present conditions and they belittle the long past conditions and thought.

The prohibition of usury belonged to the past, the practice of usury is all but universal in the present, therefore they argue that usury is a part and a necessary part of our civilization and to revive the old prohibition would turn the world's civilization backward and be as absurd as to now dispense with steam or electricity.

In reply it may be said that the changes are not universal, that there are some things that abide, that the changes are trifling when compared with those things that remain and are permanent.

1. Human nature remains the same. Man, in body and mind, in physiology and psychology, has not changed in these thousands of years. That which in ages past promoted the health and vigor

of his body, will secure its best development now. That discipline, culture and mental exercise that secured the highest intellectual strength in ages past will do the most for its best development now. Many things that now give splendor to our civilization do not promote either the best physical or mental manhood.

2. Family ties remain. The relation of husband and wife, of parents and children, and the duties of their several positions in the home have not changed. The family remains the social unit as it has been in all ages. Sociology, the science of social and political organization, is a permanent science. It does not change with the shifting temporal conditions of the people. Those things which made for the general welfare of ages ago are for the public weal now, and those things that endangered the state then are to be avoided now.

3. The moral law remains unchanged and unchangeable, with all the brilliant present there is no amendment to the ten commandments. The ethical nature remains and the voice of conscience, approving the same right and condemning the same wrong, is identical with the voice of conscience in the time of Moses.

4. The laws of nature have not changed. The relation between a cause and its sequence remains. Like causes produce like effects.

No living thing has changed its nature. A lion now is of the same nature that it was in the time of Samson. So with every savage beast that roams the jungle. Even the domesticated animals, with all the effort and skill of intelligent man, have only been smoothed or speeded a little. The horse, cow, sheep, or dog have held their old forms and dispositions.

Seed time and harvest come and go and we are dependent for the same shower and sunshine that gave Adam his first harvest.

We know some things they did not know and we have bettered our tools, but the natural world has shown no signs of change.

5. The relation of things to each other have not changed. Plants must have soil to grow in, animals must have vegetation to feed upon. Fish must have water. And so with the thousands of relations of climate, elements, soils, plants, animals, fishes, birds and insects, they are the identical relations sustained ages and ages ago.

6. The nature of money has not changed. Its material and form and denominations have been modified but the functions of money as a storage of values and as a measure of values and as a medium of exchange remain the same. Our gold and silver and paper money may be more convenient and more exact, but its functions are just the same as the Indians' wampum.

The law of supply and demand and the equity in commercial transactions, great or small, are unchanged. Money could always be used to make or gather more money in business. It is no more true now than in the times of David or Nehemiah. If this had not then been possible; if there had not been tempting opportunities, there would have been no sin of usury for them to reprove.

Man's changed conditions are but trifling and incidental, relating to himself. They do not affect a single natural or moral or economic law.

The changed conditions, which are urged as a reason that the prohibition of usury is no longer binding, are only the conditions brought about by the violation of that law.

The prohibition of usury is systematically violated. The neighbor in the smallest transaction with his neighbor exacts usury, though it be but a few cents. The credit system has become universal. It is the rare exception now to "own what you have" and to "pay as you go." Interest bearing bonds are issued by the smallest manufacturing plant, by the great corporation and by the empire. These conditions do not prove usury right. They only show how far true business, commercial, and political principles have been perverted by this practice.

If violating a law annuls it, then any law can be pushed aside. Let the claims of the Sabbath day be ignored. Let the houses of worship remain closed upon that day. Let work be planned for seven days of the week. Let the hum of the mills and the roar of commerce go on. Take no note of the Sabbath day, either in business or recreation or worship, and conditions will soon be upon us, such that we may urge as plausibly, that the Sabbath is effete, possible to our slow going fathers but inconsistent with the necessary rush of our day.

If the systematic violation of a law annuls it then we can quiet the conscience and be dishonest while dealing with a Turk in Constantinople and we may lie while dickering with a Chinese merchant in Canton.

If violating a law annuls it, even the seventh commandment, the violation of which is so offensive to decency and its observance so necessary to the purity of the home, may in this way be ruled out as a binding obligation. Let polygamy be the order, supported by the example of Jacob and David and Solomon, and the families be constituted along that line, then enforced monogamy would seem to be a sundering of tender ties and hardness toward the cast off Hagars that is inconsistent with the Christian spirit. An earnest, Godly man, a missionary friend of the writer, under whose ministry a heathen chief was converted, was misled by the plausibility. The chief had a number of wives; he had children by them; he was much attached to his wives and was fond of his children, and they all seemed to love him and clung to him. The missionary in the kindness of his heart did not interfere with the family, permitting the chief to keep his wives and placed his name on the church roll of the Mission. For this act he was reproved by the ecclesiastical authorities above him. Let polygamy become as universal as usury and even the seventh commandment in its strictness will seem impracticable and unkind if not positively cruel.

It will not do to claim freedom from the prohibition of usury because we have organized commerce and the state and all society in violation of it.

CHAPTER XIV

AMERICAN REVISION

The Revision by the American Committee is the latest effort of scholarship to bring King James' Version up to date by eliminating effete terms and using words in their modern sense.

The references to usury are here collated so as to give a general view of the question from the translations of the passages in this the latest Revision. The reader will notice that the modern word "interest" is substituted for "usury" in nearly every passage.

Exodus 22:25: "If thou lend money to any of my people with thee that is poor, thou shalt not be to him as a creditor; neither shall ye lay upon him interest."

Leviticus 25:35-37: "And if thy brother be waxen poor, and his hand fail with thee, then thou shalt uphold him: as a stranger and a sojourner shall he live with thee. Take thou no interest of him or increase, but fear thy God; that thy brother may live with thee. Thou shalt not give him thy money upon interest, nor give him thy victuals for increase."

Deuteronomy 23:19, 20: "Thou shalt not lend upon interest to thy brother: interest of money, interest of victuals, interest of anything that is lent upon interest: unto a foreigner thou mayest lend upon interest, but unto thy brother thou shalt not lend upon interest, that Jehovah thy God may bless thee in all that thou puttest thy hand unto, in the land whither thou goest in to possess it."

Nehemiah 5:7-10: "Then I consulted with myself, and contended with the nobles and rulers and said unto them, Ye exact usury, every one of his brother. And I held a great assembly against them. And I said unto them, We after our ability have redeemed our brethren the Jews that were sold unto the nations; and would ye even sell your brethren, and should they be sold unto us? Then held they their peace and found never a word. Also I said, The thing ye do is not good: ought ye not to walk in the fear of our God, because of the reproach of the nations, our enemies? And I likewise, my brethren and my servants, do lend them money and grain. I pray you, let us leave off this usury."

The interest exacted by the princes and nobles was no doubt so extortionate that it could be called usury in the modern legal sense.

Psalm 15:

"Jehovah, Who shall sojourn in thy tabernacles? Who shall dwell in thy holy hill? He that walketh uprightly and worketh righteousness, And speaketh the truth in his heart; He that slandereth not with his tongue, Nor doeth evil to his friend, Nor taketh up a reproach against his neighbor; In whose eyes a reprobate is despised, But who honoreth them that fear Jehovah; He that sweareth to his own hurt and changeth not; He that putteth not out his money to interest, Nor taketh reward against the innocent. He that doeth these things shall never be moved."

Proverbs 28:8: "He that augmenteth his substance by interest and increase, gathereth it for him that hath pity on the poor."

Jeremiah 15:10: "I have not lent, neither have men lent to me; yet every one of them doth curse me."

King James reads: "I have neither lent upon usury, nor have men lent to me upon usury." As Jeremiah was protesting his innocence of any wrongdoing the early translators inserted what was evidently implied while these latest revisors have omitted what was not in the original text.

Ezekiel 18:1-18: "The word of Jehovah came again unto me saying, What mean ye that ye use this proverb, concerning the land of Israel, saying, The fathers have eaten sour grapes and the children's teeth are set on edge? As I live saith the Lord Jehovah, ye shall not have occasion any more to use this proverb in Israel. Behold, all souls are mine, as the soul of the father so also the soul of the son is mine: the soul that sinneth, it shall die. But if a man be just and do that which is lawful and right, and hath not eaten upon the mountains, neither hath lifted up his eyes to the idols of the house of Israel, neither hath defiled his neighbor's wife, neither hath come near to a woman in her impurity, and hath not wronged any, but hath restored to the debtor his pledge, hath taken naught by robbery, hath given his bread to the hungry, and hath covered the naked with a garment: he hath not given forth upon interest, neither hath taken any increase, that hath withdrawn his hand from iniquity, hath executed true justice between man and man, hath walked in my statutes and hath kept my ordinances, to deal truly: he is just, he shall surely live, saith the Lord Jehovah.

"If he beget a son that is a robber, a shedder of blood, and that doeth any one of these things, and that doeth not any of those duties, but even hath eaten upon the mountains, and denied his neighbor's wife, hath wronged the poor and needy, hath taken by robbery, hath not restored the pledge, and hath lifted up his eyes to the idols, hath committed abomination, hath given forth upon interest, and hath taken increase; shall he then live? He shall not live: he hath done all these abominations: he shall surely die; his blood shall be upon him.

"Now, lo, if he beget a son which seeth all his father's sins which he hath done, and feareth and doeth not such like; that hath not eaten upon the mountains, neither hath lifted up his eyes to the idols of the house of Israel, hath not defiled his neighbor's wife, neither hath wronged any, hath not taken aught to pledge, neither hath taken by robbery, but hath given his bread to the hungry, and hath covered the naked with a garment; that hath not withdrawn his hand from the poor, that hath not received interest nor increase, hath executed my ordinances, hath walked in my statutes; he shall not die for the iniquity of his father, he shall surely live. As for his father, because he cruelly oppressed, robbed his brother, and did that which is not good among his people, behold, he shall die in his iniquity."

Ezekiel 22:6-12: "Behold, the princes of Israel, every one according to his power have been in thee to shed blood. In thee have they set light by father and mother; in the midst of thee have they dealt by oppression with the sojourner; in thee have they wronged the fatherless and the widow. Thou hast despised mine holy things and hast profaned my sabbaths. Slanderous men have been in thee to shed blood; and in thee have they eaten upon the mountains; in the midst of thee they have committed lewdness. In thee have they uncovered their fathers' nakedness; in thee have they humbled her that was unclean in her impurity. And one hath committed abomination with his neighbor's wife; and another hath lewdly defiled his daughter-in-law; and another in thee hath humbled his sister, his father's daughter. In thee have they taken bribes to shed blood; thou hast taken interest and increase, and thou hast greedily gained of thy neighbors by oppression and hast forgotten me saith the Lord Jehovah."

Matthew 25:26-27: "But his lord answered and said unto him, Thou wicked and slothful servant, thou knewest that I reap where I sowed not and gather where I did not scatter; thou oughtest therefore to have put my money to the bankers, and at my coming I should have received back mine own with interest."

Luke 19:22, 23: "He saith unto him, Out of thine own mouth will I judge thee, thou wicked servant. Thou knewest that I am an austere man taking up that I laid not down and reaping that I did not sow; then wherefore gavest thou not my money into the bank, and I at my coming should have required it with usury."

Luke 16:13-15: "No servant can serve two masters: for either he will hate the one, and love the other; or else he will hold to the one and despise the other. Ye cannot serve God and mammon. And the Pharisees who were lovers of money heard all these things and they scoffed at him. And he said unto them, Ye are they that justify yourselves in the sight of men but God knoweth your hearts: for that which is exalted among men is an abomination in the sight of God."

It is not easy to understand how an honest, godly man, who has even medium intelligence, unclouded by prejudice, and who has confidence in the highest scholarship of the age, can deny that the revealed Word of God, in both Testaments, condemns usury or interest. It is just as difficult to explain how any one, not glaringly inconsistent, can claim that interest taking is not a sin, who bows to the divine authority of the revealed Word and who defines sin as "Any want of conformity unto or transgression of the law of God."

CHAPTER XV

DUTY LEARNED FROM TWO SOURCES

In this discussion we learn our duty from two sources. Two authorities are recognized. One is the revelation of God in his written Word. The other is the book of nature; this includes the ethical nature of man, his social relations, and the laws that govern material things.

The author of the Bible is the God of nature. They are but two volumes from the same mind and hand. They must speak in harmony when both are understood. Truth found in the inspired Word cannot be contradicted in nature; and no facts in the works of God can be found in conflict with the Word He has spoken. A truth found in either is always consistent with the truths made plain in the other.

Familiarity with one prepares us to better understand the other. The devout student of the Word has his mind aroused, and his susceptibility so quickened that he is able to read more clearly the lessons in the volumes of nature open before him. The student of nature, who has searched its mysteries and taken in its beauty and designs of infinite wisdom everywhere appearing, must be the more ready and competent to appreciate the revealed love and grace.

The Bible is not a treatise on natural science, nor does natural science teach revealed religion, yet they do not conflict. The special student of either may have perfect confidence that whatever he has found true in his chosen field will be found consistent with truth in other fields of special study.

Chemistry, biology and all studies of nature, are found only to give a higher conception of the God of all grace. The same wisdom and power shine out in His works that are revealed in His Word.

Again, the laws of God, whether fixed in nature or revealed in His Word, are for the highest interest of the physical, mental and spiritual man. Every truth in the Word works for the welfare of man's body and soul. The laws of nature, physical and psychological, obeyed, promote man's bodily and mental vigor. Strict obedience to the laws of God, as revealed in both Word and nature, produces the completest physical and mental manhood.

God had the highest welfare of every man at heart when He prepared the earth for his abode and gave him dominion over it. And He yearned for his deliverance from a fallen estate when He gave him a revelation of His infinite redeeming love. The eye of God is upon each individual of the race, as upon every sparrow. He has in thought, in word and in works, not the favoring of one of an hundred, while the ninety and nine are crushed or neglected, but the happiness and highest good of every one of the hundred.

The ethics of the Bible and the ethics of nature, as wrought out by the earnest heathen philosophers, mainly agree. It is an astonishment to some that there is so much agreement in the systems of heathen morals and the revealed moral law. The moral law is written on men's hearts, and can be read there by the diligent and careful student; but the consciences of men, enlightened and quickened by the revealed Word, produce the highest ethical types the world knows.

The Bible is not a work on political economy, yet there is nothing out of harmony with the most perfect political institutions. When we find political principles clearly revealed, we shall find the same truths when we study the most orderly relations of men in their social organization.

The Bible is not a work on economics, yet it advances no economic principles that work a hardness or injustice to any. When we find economic principles clearly stated, we shall surely find the same truths confirmed in a careful study of the nature of things.

As the written Word forbids usury or interest, it can be presumed that the nature of things and man's highest good also forbids it; that it is not an arbitrary prohibition, but is given in love because it is in its very nature a ruinous evil. As we find a positive prohibition of taking usury or interest in the old dispensation and the confirmation of it in the new, both by the words of the Master and the understanding and practice of the disciples and fathers, we may confidently expect that it will be confirmed by a correct and careful study of ethics and of the relation of man to things.

We may learn duty from either or both sources. To some men the Bible comes with the greatest clearness and the utmost force of authority. Others find in nature their highest conception of the Infinite, and their best directions for a correct life. If usury or interest is found to be a sin from the Word, there is no need for those to enter into the economic proof who have no taste for this character of study or reasoning. If it is found to be *"malum per se"* from the nature of things, even those who reject the divine revelation must array themselves against it. If it is shown to be evil by both revelation and economic law, then all peoples, Christian and heathen, should combine against it.

CHAPTER XVI

RIGHTS OF MAN OVER THINGS

Man was the last and the crowning work of the Creator. God made man in his own image and gave him dominion over all creatures.

"For thou hast made him a little lower than the angels, and hast crowned him with glory and honor.

"Thou madest him to have dominion over the works of thy hands; thou hast put all things under his feet:

"All the sheep and oxen, yea, and the beasts of the field;

"The fowl of the air, and the fish of the sea, and whatsoever passeth through the paths of the seas."

This high position is in entire harmony with man's innate consciousness of his superior powers, and of his nobler spiritual nature, and of his rightful dominion over all the other material creations. Man is a person, a thinking intelligent being, and is conscious of his personality, and from his lofty height he calls all else the lower and the inferior creatures. Wherever man is found over the whole earth, of whatever faith or grade of civilization, he claims this universal dominion.

Man was commanded to subdue the earth and bring it into subjection as his servant and he is conscious of his right to use all things to promote his comfort, convenience and welfare.

Anything he can make of service to himself he has a right to appropriate.

A tree is a thing which he may prepare for his own purposes, for fuel, for tools, or for a dwelling, as he pleases.

Isaiah ridiculed the idolater in his time, who made an idol of wood and worshiped it, while with another part of the same tree he built a fire and warmed himself. A part he served and a part served him. The whole tree was subject to him; in itself it had no rights.

Rights belong to persons, and not to things, and personality cannot be transferred to a thing. If there is no personal owner the question of rights is never raised. The tree, or any thing whatever, has no rights in the matter. Rights belong to the owner, the person, not to the thing he owns.

The game in the mountain forests and the fish in the rivers are things with no owner and whosoever will may take and use them.

Land is a thing, and any person may make it into a farm or garden and build upon it his home. The land has no rights and makes no protest. The whole earth is subject to man and is to be subdued by him. If no owner appears his rights are not disputed. Our fathers found an unowned continent, with all its rich resources of soil and forests and mines. It was to them free, and with the labor of a few generations they transformed it into farms and plantations and built it over with magnificent cities.

Even that which formerly was the property of another has no rights. The deserted hunter's hut in the mountains can be appropriated. The abandoned farm does not resist a new tenant. A derelict vessel, still afloat but driven before the winds, whose officers, crew and owners are at the bottom of the sea, can be appropriated, for there is no one to dispute the claim.

Even force or labor in the abstract is but a thing and has no rights. The wind is unowned and any one who will may harness it to do his work. The electric forces of nature are unowned, whoever will may gather and direct them to do his purpose. The waterfall may be made to do man's work and will not resist. The animals have no rights against man. The broncho, horse, ox, mule, or animal of any kind, may be turned to man's service. All the forces of nature were made for man. They have no rights to be regarded, when his interests can be served.

It is man's high privilege to stand above all things, to call them to his feet and to compel their service. It is the reversion of the order for him to take the subordinate place and serve the inferior creation. Things subdued, such as wealth secured, is to minister to his highest good and to promote his noblest manhood. The order is reversed when this wealth commands his service and sacrifice. The miser both reverses the divine order and violates common sense by giving the love and service of his shriveling soul to a thing.

The usurer and the borrower on usury, both, reverse the true order by assuming that a thing can claim man's service. Both grant that a thing has rights to be respected. The usurer takes the service as due to the thing he owns. It is his property that is exalted, and for which he claims the service must be rendered, and if the borrower will think closely, he will find that in paying usury he is serving a thing.

A man reverses the divine order and degrades himself, and becomes a gross idolater, when he serves things unowned instead of commanding their service, "stocks and stones." He reverses the true order when he becomes a miser and serves that which is his own, "which his own fingers have made," instead of compelling it to serve him. He is not less degraded when he exalts over himself a thing owned by another and serves it. The ownership of another does not change the nature of the thing. One can serve his neighbor's idol as truly as he can his own.

There is nothing above man but God. His fellow man is by his side, his equal, and all other material creations are beneath his feet, and he is not to permit his fellow man to lift up the inferior thing and place it above him. If he does he must step down from the pinnacle on which he was placed by his God and which his own consciousness demands he shall occupy.

"Shall the ax boast itself against him that heweth therewith? or shall the saw magnify itself against him that shaketh it? as if the rod should shake itself against them that lift it up, or as if the staff should lift up itself, as if it were no wood." Isaiah 10:15.

If he serves the borrowed ax and saw for the claim that the ax and saw have against him, he admits his debt to things and Isaiah's ridicule of an idolater can be turned against him and he steps down from the position of conscious inborn dignified lordship and becomes a servant of the inferior things.

CHAPTER XVII

EQUAL RIGHTS OF MEN

All men have sacred rights that must be regarded. That these rights are equal is so familiar and stale an expression that it hardly need be spoken. "All men are created equal," each having rights, that are inalienable, and each having the right to resist the encroachment on his rights by another. To protect these rights governments are instituted.

The vital energy of a man is his own and his right to it must be regarded. Since the abolition of chattel slavery this has been indefeasible except for crime.

He has a right to his own vital energy and to all that his own vital force produces. He has a right to his property inherited, earned, or however secured, except by fraud. He has no claim against the vital energy of his fellow man, nor has he any claim whatever against the property of another.

The working man needs capital. His vital energy must waste unless there is material upon which it may be expended. There must be the tree, land or material in some form, upon which he can work. But give him the world raw and unsubdued and he can transform it again as he has. He can build again everything on land and sea, the farms, towns, and cities, and the floating palaces. He can again dig out the mines and refine the silver and gold, mould the clay, smelt the ore and shape the iron. His needs and his power, however, give him no claim to the property of another.

The man of property is dependent upon the laborer. He may be the owner of farms, forests and mines, of horses, flocks and herds, of railroads and oil wells, yet these will not minister to him nor serve him without the laborer. His coffers may be filled with gold, and his barns bursting with grain and his stalls filled with fatlings, yet all this wealth is useless and lost, unless touched with the vital energy of an intelligent laborer. But his dependence and losses give him no right to the labor of another.

He has no right, no just claim, to the services of another man, his equal. All his wealth cannot confer the right. Wealth is but a thing, in itself without rights, and can therefore add nothing to the rights of its owner.

He may however use his wealth to command service by might, but not by right. A club is but a thing having no will and no rights, yet in the hands of a savage it adds greatly to his power and may be used by him to oppress another of his tribe. A ruffian with his gun meeting a defenseless man may so command him, that he is ready for the most abject obedience. An armed highwayman may compel a brave man "to stand and deliver." So a man may use his property to secure the service of another but it gives him no right to that service.

The usurer, who has himself no rights against his fellows, uses a thing, his property, as an instrument or weapon to command service.

He may place his hand upon every material thing another must have, and withhold it, and the other is shut up and compelled, he has no alternative. He must yield to the demands or suffer. Many men are driven to the last extremity before they will borrow.

But if the borrower is very willing and urgent for the loan, this does not change the nature of the act. The game may be shot upon the wing as it is endeavoring to escape, or it may be snared in a trap by a tempting bait. The wild broncho may be captured in chase, or beguiled into the corral.

The voluntary sacrifice of others to the usurer does not make his gains just. The foolish ones are now willing to invest in lottery tickets, yet that does not make the lottery lawful. Slot machines are being put out of the cities, because so many are ready to part with their nickels. If there were none ensnared by them, they could stand harmless.

The borrower may be greatly elated with the hope of gain, but the injustice is the same, whether the services be secured by compelling force, or by guile, or by the folly of the victim.

If we admit the supremacy of man over the material creation, all subordinate to him, and no right to be, except to serve him, and also admit the equal rights of all men, there is no escape from the conclusion that the usurer can have no rightful claims to any portion of the labor of the borrower, without surrendering to him some portion of his property as compensation for the services received. He must have less property when the service is rendered and the borrower must have more property if the rights of both are regarded.

A false impression prevails, that the lender in some way gives the loan to the borrower; that the borrower becomes somewhat the owner of the property. The borrower is encouraged in this illusion and it becomes a plausible basis for the claim upon his services.

When a loan is made to a bank it is called a "deposit" and rightly, for it is only placed in the banker's hands and does not in any part become his. This is true of any amount, great or small, whether the deposit draws interest or not. The lender never loses his sense of ownership of the whole amount, nor does the banker encourage the fiction that he has become part owner.

Every loan is but a "deposit." The ownership of no part passes to the borrower. It is seldom that the loan or "deposit" is not safer in the keeping of the borrower than in the hands of the owner himself, when secured by mortgages or personal sureties. The usurer gains the earnings of the borrower but parts with no property. He receives the service but gives nothing.

Two usurers, A and B, are neighbors. A has a garden he wishes dug. He has an ax but no hoe. B has wood that he wishes cut. He has a hoe but no ax. The laborer appears and wishes to do their work. Usurer A agrees to lend him his ax to cut B's wood on the condition that he shall return it unimpaired and work his garden for its use.

He cuts the wood, but has no hoe to dig A's garden for the use of the ax. Usurer B now lends the laborer his hoe to dig the garden, but takes the cutting of the wood for the use of the hoe. The confused borrower knows he is defrauded of his work, though each seems to have a plausible claim upon him.

A does not give the hoe to the laborer. He retains the full ownership but deposits it in the workman's hands to be returned unimpaired. B does not give away his ax, he only places it in the laborer's hands also to be returned unimpaired. The full hoe and full ax is returned and they have taken the services without compensation.

The result is just the same as if A and B had traded tools and A had given the laborer a hoe to dig the garden, "the tool and the material with which to work," and B had given him an ax to cut his wood, "the tool and the material with which to work," without a pretense of a payment for his labor.

Taking only a part of the borrower's or laborer's services does not relieve it of injustice. The nature of the oppression is the same, only less heinous and flagrant. He who took a penny belonging to another is a thief as truly as the man who took a pound. Petit larceny and grand larceny differ only in the amount stolen. The man who takes three per cent. of the labor of another wrongfully defrauds as the man who takes fifty per cent. The nature of the wrong is the same; they only differ in degree.

It is a well known fact, however, often repeated, that ninety-five out of every hundred who go into business with borrowed capital, that is, who pay interest on "their material and tools," do give the vigor of their lives to the service of usurers and at the end have nothing.

The element of time is only a figment that clouds the question of right and deceives the borrower. In order that the labor of another may be appropriated it is necessary to give him time to work. The laborer may dig in A's garden a day or all summer and he may chop wood for B a day or all winter. The result is the same. It is necessary that the borrower be given time to earn something before it is or can be appropriated. The question is, how rapidly can he earn, and how soon can his earnings be collected? Long time loans with the frequent payments of the earnings of the victim are the ideal conditions of the usurer.

CHAPTER XVIII

A FALSE BASAL PRINCIPLE

That usury or interest must be held under the restraints of law is recognized in nearly all countries. It is treated as a necessary evil that cannot be abolished, and therefore must be controlled. Bacon said, "It is permitted on account of the hardness of men's hearts."

The laws differ in the various states. The rate of interest authorized by a particular state is not invariably fixed, but is changed as the condition of the people seems to demand.

That which determines the rate, of any particular people, at any particular time, is the productive ability of the borrower. The rate now in England is about three per cent. The conditions being such that the productive power of the borrower is very limited. In the United States, where the natural resources are not all occupied, and the avenues for successful effort more numerous, the average is seven per cent. In the western states of the United States the rates are higher than in the eastern, for the material resources lie so open and undeveloped that the productive power of the borrower is far greater than in the older eastern states.

The basal for the rate of interest is the benefit or the advantage of the loan to the borrower. What can the borrower do or make with this capital? How great a benefit can he gain by it? The rate is based on the earnings of the borrower.

The transfer from R. R. station to R. R. station across this city is twenty-five cents. That I may make my train and meet my appointment, that prompt and rapid transfer is of greater value to me, but that does not give the hackman the right to an increased charge.

The fare to the distant city is ten dollars, but to me, with important business waiting and suffering, it is worth an hundred. The conductor does not ask me what my profits are to be from this trip. He collects the same fare of all for the same service, whatever their interests may be in the passage.

The letter which is freighted with a proposition that affects my future life is two cents. Because of great value to me the postal service is no more than a letter of idle gossip.

Railroad freight rates are at times arbitrarily fixed on the basis of the benefit to the patron. The rates of freight from a coal mine are sometimes made by a railroad on the basis of the profits of operating the mine. The rates to a quartz mine in the mountains are often so regulated. A contractor, dependent on a transportation company, must often share his profits. Such rates are regarded as unjust and oppressive and efforts are made to correct the evil by law.

A is crossing the city and can without inconvenience carry a note to a party for B. That accommodation without sacrifice or inconvenience on the part of A is no basis for a charge upon B, though the delivery of the message was of value to B, but if A discovers that in delivering that note he can make it a matter of business gain to himself, that would not justify B in claiming a part of the profits A secured for himself. While A served his own business he also favored B. It would be unreasonable and unjust for B to forget the favor and make a charge against A, because in the delivery of the note A managed to gain a profit.

Two farmers are without barns. It will require the labor of a number of years to secure the requisite amount of lumber and other material to enable them to erect their barns. One of the farmers undertakes to shelter and protect from decay the lumber of both, until the requisite amount can be secured. This is a real favor to the other and is accepted readily. He even offers to pay him for the care and liability. But he discovers afterward that his neighbor, by wise, careful and skillful piling, has made from this lumber a shelter for his stock and grain. That he has so managed as to gain for himself a benefit. Then, with the false principle of usury he makes a charge for the keeping of the very thing for which he was willing to pay a price.

A gentleman not wanting his coach for a time, but wishing it to be kept in perfect repair, and his team fed and exercised, to be kept sleek and strong, leaves it in his coachman's care. The coachman agrees to keep from decay, and to replace should one die, and at the end of the term, return the coach in perfect condition, no mar or wear, and the team sleek and strong from good care, feed and daily exercise. But the coachman discovers that in the daily exercise of the team he can carry a party of business men to and from their offices, and secure for himself a gain. He, at the end of the term, returns the carriage and equipage complete as he received it. The owner has had his property perfectly cared for during the term he could not use it. But the owner learning of the benefit to the keeper, which would not have been possible without his equipage, demands a portion of the benefit which cost him nothing, nor in the least diminished his property.

A gentleman has a warm, rich and beautiful robe, but is about to travel a number of years among the countries of Cuba, Porto Rico, and the Philippines, where he will not need it, and afterward visit Siberia, where he will need and use it. Another undertakes to relieve him of all care of it during these years and deliver it to the Siberian home ready for his use. He protects it

111

from the moths in summer, and guards it against all touch or taint, and delivers it in the perfect condition in which it was received. In justice he deserves a reward from the owner, and if he received no benefit, would receive it, but it is found that he needed it for his comfort by the way, and that without it he should have perished. Then the owner demands a reward for the benefit the carrier received. The owner did no service. He received a positive benefit, but the porter, who carried the burden all the way, must pay interest or rental because he was kept from perishing by it.

The surprise or discovery feature is introduced into the above illustrations to emphasize the false basis upon which the rates of interest rest. In the actual practice of usury the lender may have full information as to the use of the loan and its advantages to the borrower. If we eliminate this feature the basis still remains untenable. By no tortion of ethics can I demand that he, who does me a favor, shall pay me for the privilege.

A man has one thousand dollars of money he is not using. He gives it to another to keep or place in a drawer in his vault. To care for this and be responsible for it, a commission is allowed, for it is no benefit to the keeper. Even an amount is asked for the drawer in the vault, without responsibility. To care for this a term of years is deserving of a reward. But now keeping the property equally safe, and returning every dollar when the owner calls for it, is not satisfactory to the usurer. If this money has in any way proved a benefit to the keeper, through his wisdom and energy and skill, he demands an increase. What is this loan worth to you? is the question of the usurer to the borrower.

The basis of legal interest rates is the amount of benefit the borrower gains by the loan. If his opportunities in a state are favorable, and he may by diligence make a large gain, the rates are high. If in another state his opportunities are so limited that, strive as he may, he can make little gain, the legal rates will be low.

The basis is so absurd that many have urged the repeal of all laws regulating the rates of interest. "Why should the laws presume to level the rates for a whole state? The possibilities and opportunities of gain are infinitely varied. Every borrower knows his own conditions and the amount of advantage the loan is to him and he should be permitted to pay for money whatever he is willing to pay."

One writer thus expresses it, "No man of ripe years and of sound mind, acting freely, and with his eyes open, ought to be hindered, with a view to his advantage, from making such bargains in the way of obtaining money, as he thinks fit; nor anybody hindered from supplying him upon any terms he thinks proper to accede to."

Jeremy Bentham is often quoted to prove the absurdity of all laws regulating the rates of interest, and yet all his elaborate arguments are based on this false principle.

If usury is wrong only when the borrower can make no profit, and is right whenever the borrower can make a gain by it, and the rate of interest is to be measured by that gain, then all laws are illogical that limit the rate, and may be classed among those restraining trade.

CHAPTER XIX

THE TRUE ETHICAL PRINCIPLE

The true ethical principle that should govern the relation between the owner of property and the person holding that property as a loan, does not differ from the principle that is recognized as prevailing in all the other relations of life. The party to whom the service is rendered is under obligation. The party served is the one who must pay for the service. The party served must pay in proportion to the amount of service rendered him. If that service is great, then the payment must be large. If the service is slight, then the payment is small, and when there is no service then no payment can be claimed.

This principle is recognized in all worthy and upright transactions. It is the service rendered that is rewarded in a court of justice. An employe recovers his wages from his employer for his services rendered. The condition of the employer's business does not enter into the count. It may have been unprofitable or a great success but that cannot affect the claim either way.

A physician charges for the services given a patient. The recovery or death of the patient can neither increase nor diminish them.

In service we always surrender something of ourselves or of our own, and each knows the sacrifice or effort he has made; he cannot know the value of this to the other, and he need not know. Full compensation is due from the party served but no compensation is due when no service is given nor property surrendered.

The usurer's whole claim is for the service of his property. But he does not surrender a particle of his wealth. He does not become poorer in making his loan. He holds all his wealth as fully as before, whether it be a loan of money or grains or tools. There has been no outgo of property for which, in any other relation, he could claim a reward or compensation from his fellow. He simply deposits his property with his fellow and takes security for its safe keeping. It must be preserved perfectly and restored fully.

When we consider the true principle, that compensation is due always for services rendered, the obligation is upon the lender for the care and preservation of his property. The borrower in any and every case gives a real and valuable service in preservation and restoration at the end of the term, while the lender renders no personal service nor does he part with a particle of his wealth.

There is always a service rendered in caring for and preserving the property of another. It may be very great or it may be very small. It may be so great that no one would undertake it though the property should be freely given him.

In 1800 the "Faithful Steward" was wrecked in Delaware bay near the shore. It had on board a large number of passengers, emigrants, who nearly all perished. Few lives were saved and all the property was lost. One young man, of the kin of the writer, swam ashore through the breakers. Before he left the vessel an old man offered him a stocking full of gold if he cared to try and save it. Though young and vigorous he would not undertake to try to save it for it. This was an extreme case of risk and danger.

In another extreme case the service may be very small, reduced to the minimum, for instance, caring for the gold of another by locking it up in a fire and burglar-proof safe. For this simple service a comparatively small charge is made. But caring for the property of another is always some service that earns a reward great or small.

The nature of the service is not changed and the principle still holds when the deposit is made with a person who gives ample pledges for its full return; the principle still holds when the deposit is made in a farm and secured there by mortgage, making it safer than in the iron vault.

The true ethical principle, equity between man and man, requires that the holder of the property of another shall be compensated by the owner of the property for his services in caring for and preserving it. The amount of compensation depends on the difficult or favorable conditions attending its care. These conditions greatly vary, perhaps in no two cases are exactly alike, and so there can be no fixed price or rate at which one will receive and care for the property of another. The extreme limit of liberality permitted is that he may care for the property of another for nothing. He is not permitted to pay a price for the privilege. The revealed divine law, true ethics and equity and duty of self preservation forbid him. Perfect preservation of any amount, large or small, for any time, long or short, whatever the incidental advantages to the borrower, is the highest compensation a borrower is permitted to give for any loan. The demand for more than this by the owner is to be resisted as unjust and oppressive.

An express company receives a package of money for which it receipts and becomes responsible and agrees to deliver to the owner at some distant point. For this service it receives compensation in accordance with the amount of service. If the conditions are dangerous and the distance great the charge is large. If the conditions are very favorable and safe the charges are small.

If the amount of service is reduced to the minimum, in rare cases, no charge may be made. But that a price should be paid for the privilege of caring for and conveying it, is inconsistent with the management of an honest business. The purpose would be either to rob the owner of his wealth or to rob the employes of their services.

An insurance company undertakes to protect a property for a term of years, to a distant date. A rate is given for protection from a single element, as fire. If all destructive agents are included the rate is higher. The rate is higher for a long than a short period. All the business world recognize the value of this service and nearly every kind of property may now be insured. The premium is cheerfully paid by the owner of the property for the service rendered him. It is a real and valuable service to have his property protected, preserved, or restored, so that it cannot be lost before the distant date. It is conceivable that a property might be so indestructible that the risk would be practically nothing and a policy might be issued without a premium, but that a price should be paid for the privilege of protecting any property is utterly inconsistent with rational insurance.

Now usury presumes to reverse this ethical order and requires that the insurance company shall pay the owner of the property for the privilege of protecting it. Under usury the property given into the care of another, and called a loan, must be perfectly protected and preserved by the borrower, restored if lost, and returned in full to the owner at the agreed distant date, and a price paid for the privilege of performing the service.

The true ethical principle and equity in the relations between the owner of a property and the one who holds, protects and preserves it, require that the owner shall render to the holder a just compensation. This will vary in different conditions, it may be very small, it may in rare cases be entirely eliminated; but they also utterly forbid that the party rendering the service shall pay for the privilege of serving.

One may submit to an injustice in order to gain an advantage. He can do better for himself by submitting than by resisting. His employer may be hard and oppressive but this is the best job he can get and he holds on, but that does not justify the oppressions of the employer up to the breaking point. It may be to the advantage of a borrower to submit to the exactions of usury, that is, he may gain more wealth by borrowing upon interest than not, but that does not relieve usury of its oppression up to the breaking point when it can no longer be endured. There is no better ethical basis for low interest than high interest. Low rates of interest are oppressions that may be suffered or endured for a possible gain, but high rates are intolerable. The principle is the same whatever the rate of interest, whether it be low or high. They only differ in the degrees of their severity.

CHAPTER XX

WEALTH IS BARREN

That wealth can produce wealth is the assumption of Shylock.

Shylock—"When Jacob grazed his Uncle Laban's sheep—
This Jacob from our holy Abraham was
The third possessor; ay, he was the third."
Antonio—"And what of him? Did he take interest?"
Shylock—"No, not take interest; not as you would say,
Directly interest. Mark what Jacob did." * * *
Antonio—"This was a venture, sir, that Jacob served for;
A thing not in his power to bring to pass—
But swayed and fashioned by the hand of Heaven.
Was this inserted to make interest good?
Or is your gold and silver, ewes and rams?"
Shylock—"I can not tell; I make them breed as fast."
—*Merchant of Venice.*

It is only intelligent energy that can produce wealth. Even the natural resources must be subdued and shaped by intelligent energy to be of service to man. Trees do not betake themselves into the form of houses. Land does not transform itself into farms and gardens. Coal does not come to our fires without hands. Ore is not iron, nor is clay pottery. They must be carefully manipulated by the intelligent laborer.

Nothing man can make has the power of self propagation. All wealth is as barren as silver and gold, though Shylock claimed he could make them breed like ewes and rams. Life alone is productive, and the secrets of life man has not touched.

A tree or animal grows by the life that is in it, but the accretions of wealth are from the efforts of intelligent energy outside of itself. Wealth is an effect, a result. The vital energy of a person, of "a willing intelligent being" produces wealth, but it does not follow that it has the qualities of its cause. It has no intelligence, nor has it self-determining power, nor is it vital, nor has it energy, it has not in itself the force to overcome its inertia, the energy must be applied. It has no power to increase or grow. A fortune is built, as a building is built, brick after brick is added by intelligent hands.

All wealth must have the living hands applied to cause it to increase even the smallest amount. There is no such thing as "productive" capital. It is so called when it is used to gather and appropriate the earnings of others, but wealth in none of its forms has the quality or power of producing.

Money, the most familiar form, is barren. A bag of dollars stored for ages will not have increased a single coin. No one holds or handles money on the assumption that it will increase in his hands. Money is a care, and the broker who holds or handles it relies for his compensation, not on the increase of the dollars in his hands, but on the increase from some producer to whom he lends it. If there is no borrower he takes a direct commission from the amount itself, as trustee or administrator or custodian.

Money is readily exchanged for any other property. Money has a number of functions but in exchange it is a medium by which the value of articles is conveyed. It takes the place of the bags which conveyed the wheat, of the crates which contained the potatoes, of the baskets which carried the peaches, and the wrapping which held the cotton or the wool.

Col. Irish, who was chief of the Bureau of Engraving and Printing at Washington, when he died, and under whose administration the present building was erected, at one time sent to the wife of the writer a ten dollar bill, wrapped up so that it looked like a picture, cabinet size; this was accompanied by a note, to be opened first. In this note he said he took pleasure in sending her an excellent likeness of our late lamented president, which he would be pleased to have her accept. If she should prefer it in some other form, it was a peculiarity of this likeness that it would change instantly at the will of the holder into any form desired; that this was the peculiarity that troubled him, as he had been unable to decide what would please her best, and had finally decided to send it in this form, and let her change it into any other she might like better.

Money is a peculiar medium which will hold and carry the value of anything. You pour in your wheat and take it to the merchant, who empties your wheat and fills it with clothes, he carries it to the dealer in any article needed and the vessel is instantly emptied and refilled.

The values of the products of laborers in the various occupations of life or the products of the various climates are thus readily exchanged by money, but the gain is not in the money. The art in trade is to study and know the products and needs of the laborers of one class or country, and the varied products and needs of the producers of another class or local community. The skill in trade is in supplying the needs of one from the products of the other.

The profit in trade is the gain from securing for an article a greater portion of the product of those whose needs are supplied, than was given to those who produced it. The harvester cost the manufacturer twenty days' work. The farmer, who needs and purchases it, pays forty days' work for it. The farmer may produce one hundred bushels of wheat with twenty-five days' work, but the mechanics in the city, who need it for bread, may give twice that amount of labor for that quantity of wheat. There is a wide field for skill and profit in trade, when the products and needs of all classes and all lands are considered. But money does not add to wealth in trade. There is nothing produced by it in trade. It is but the tool by which values are conveyed, and no more productive than baskets or crates or sacks. Intelligent energy produces all the profits that are secured by trading.

Modern apologists for usury, knowing that money is unproductive itself, call it a tool for production, and as it can be readily transformed into any tool, they try to avoid the logical conclusion that the taking of interest on money is unjust and oppressive to the producer.

But no tool is productive. All tools are but the reaching out of man for the better control and mastery of material things.

The tool is but dead matter; the productive efficiency is in the vital energy of the intelligent laborer. The most complicated and ingenious tool ever made is useless without the operator. It is as helpless as the wire without the electric current; as helpless as the body without its life, for the body is but man's tool, preserved, and kept efficient, and made productive, by the living energy alone.

Tools are but the reaching out of the vital energy beyond the body. Tools are but the means, invented and constructed, by which the man can overcome his physical limitations and accomplish wonders, the impossible to a creature wanting in his intelligence.

These glasses enable dim eyes to see clearly. There is no ability in the glasses to see; they would be of no use on blind eyes. I see, these spectacles cannot see. Enlarge and so place these lenses that I can see bacteria, or the mountains of the moon, yet this microscope or this telescope has no more life nor sight than this single lens. I, with it, see the minute creation or examine the distant planet. It is but the extension of my eye.

This pen and paper and this book are but the means by which I reach and reason with my fellow-men. They are but my tools to convey my thought. I am reasoning with you, not this paper and ink.

My hand is the natural tool with which I labor. I may work in the garden and plant the seed and destroy the weeds with my hand alone, and there is no dispute but that I do the work. I take a small weeder in my hand and greatly increase my efficiency. I take a hoe and reach out further and greatly add to my efficiency. I am the efficient agent. There is no power in the weeder or the hoe. I take my plow, as my tool, and I tear up the soil and prepare it for my harvest. I take the complicated harvester and gather it into my barn. In every part of that process the tool is but the reaching out of my energy beyond my body. There is no place where that tool becomes vitalized and productive.

I am a porter, I carry packages in my hands. To increase my efficiency I build me a cart, and smooth a roadway, by which I am able to carry more and heavier packages with ease. I construct a roadway across the continent, and with the power which I employ I carry the commerce of the nation. I build ships and direct them from continent to continent and handle the commerce of the world. Now there is no place from this simple carriage in the hand, to the complicated and stupendous system of transportation, where the tool is not wholly dependent on the vital intelligent energy.

When the vital principle leaves this body, then hands, eyes and the whole body is helpless. Withdraw the vital energy from these means by which man extends his power beyond the body, and all the implements of agriculture will not produce a harvest, and the wheels of commerce on land and sea would instantly stop.

There is no place in the most complicated machine where it begins to produce. The machine may show the greatest ingenuity in its invention and the perfection of skill in its construction, and the intelligence necessary to its operation may be reduced to the minimum, yet no where and at no time can it produce of itself.

When a criminal is arraigned in court the responsibility is placed upon the person, the intelligent energy, always. It matters not by what tools the burglary or other criminal act was committed. The man who handled the tools is held accountable for the results. His tools may show the greatest ingenuity and the highest skill in their construction but they do not share his guilt. He is the efficient and responsible cause. If this were not so justice could be so perverted that the preservation of the order and the security of society would be impossible.

Every tool is itself produced, and its maker must be rewarded or paid once, but there the claim for the tool ends. The laborer who constructs the machine cannot demand repayment over and over. The skilled mechanic who produced this pair of lenses must be paid, but he has no claim for second payment. To secure repayment he must make another pair. The maker of this pen and this paper must be paid, but that ends his claim. The maker of the hoe or cart or engine must have the reward he has earned, but can prefer no second claim.

There is no question when the laborer makes and owns his own tool. The labor of constructing the tool must be rewarded as well as the laborer in its operation.

When the tools are complicated and require the skill of many, the makers of the machine are usually different persons from the laborers who operate it. In this case the payment of all must come from the finished product. Those who constructed the machine and those who operate it must be paid by the consumers.

If the shoe plant is built and operated, then from the shoes produced must come the payment for all. The workmen who built the plant and the engines and machinery for the manufacture of the different parts of the shoe, must be paid by the consumer of shoes. The workmen who built the plant must be as fully compensated as those who operate it, but being compensated, they have no claim for recompensation for the same work. To be paid again they must build a new plant. The operators must be compensated for every shoe they make, but they can not reclaim payment over and over again. To receive more pay they must make more shoes.

Both classes of laborers have a right to full compensation for all the labor performed. Neither party has a right to demand a second payment for the same labor.

It would be manifestly as unjust for the constructors of the plant to compel the operators to pay them over and over again, as it would be for the operators of the machine, having supplied the community with shoes, to demand payment over and over without making another shoe. The shoes will wear out, so will the machines. It is as unreasonable for the first class of laborers to compel the operators of their machinery to keep the same in repair, as for the operators to compel their customers to keep their shoes in perfect condition. For the first laborers to receive a new payment they must build a new plant, and for the operators to receive a new payment they must make new shoes.

The confusion of ideas comes in when there intervenes a third party between these two classes of laborers. This third party meets the demands of the class of laborers who build the plant and machines, from hoarded wealth, and then exacts payment from those who operate it. This is then called productive capital, but it is no more productive than the money in the bank vault. The producing, so called, is but the exacting of a part of that which the operators produce. It is the exacting of payment that never pays. The operators are compelled to be forever buying, yet the plant is never bought. The capitalist is forever selling, yet the plant is never sold.

Usually, the usurer is a fourth party that stands yet behind the third party, taking no risks, demanding complete security for his loan and also an increase out of the products of the operators. The third party assumes all care and guarantees against all losses and depends for his compensation on a portion of the product after the demands of the fourth party are satisfied. This third party may be an active producer. All that he receives may be fully earned in care, oversight and management of the business of the plant.

But the fourth party can have no claim for his services, he has no part in the production. The absurdity, the figment that his capital is productive, is introduced to cover the evident fraud of appropriating, without compensation, a portion of the products of the operators. He has no more claim to an increase of his capital year by year and a doubling in a term of years, than the laborers who built it have to the same plant, perfect and unworn at the end of a term, and in addition, another plant equal in every respect. They built but one, they have no claim upon a second. For the usurer, who takes their place, to double his wealth, and yet the debt be undischarged, is a flagrant fraud.

The underlying falsehood is that wealth changes its nature when put in the hands of a live man and becomes productive. It is acknowledged that wealth lying in the vault is barren and at the same time it is claimed that it produces in the hands of an intelligent agent. But it is the same dead, helpless, barren thing wherever it may be found and whatever form it may be made to take. The dollar taken from the vault and exchanged for a hoe does not receive this new quality. The hoe is as dead as the dollar. When this hoe is in the hands of the workman it is the same barren thing is was before he picked it up. These glasses are precisely the same when astride my nose as when lying on the table. It is not true that wealth in any form, though it be that of a useful tool, takes on this new quality or attribute when in the hands of a live man.

A man's labor is more productive with suitable tools than without them. The same energy will secure far greater returns. If it were not so he would not trouble to make tools or use them. But to call tools productive agents and so reward them is to rob intelligent energy, skill and inventive genius of that which they alone can produce. This degrades the man to the level of the tool or exalts the tool to the height of its maker.

CHAPTER XXI

WEALTH DECAYS

All man-made wealth is subject to inevitable decay. Aristotle said, "Labor produces all wealth," but the product has no sooner left the laborer's hands than it begins to perish. The vital energy that produced it must follow to preserve it from the ravages of time.

Take the life, the vital part, from the body, and corruption begins. So with all that has been produced, withdraw the vital force and ruin immediately follows. The vital energy must ever be present and active to preserve it.

Fruits and grains and provisions of all kinds for human food rapidly perish. The laborer must be continually active, producing and preserving, or the race would be starving in a fortnight. Even the miraculously bestowed manna became corrupt in a night. It had to be gathered day by day.

Flocks and herds need the shepherd's care. They are subject to disease and natural enemies and are short lived, so that however large and strong, and healthy the herd of cattle, or the flock of sheep, it would be soon scattered and lost to the owner without watchful care.

Tools and instruments of production, great or small, if used, soon need to be renewed, or if unused perish even sooner. Neglected they speedily decay. The locomotive left unattended on the track would soon be utterly useless from the destructive elements of rain and heat, frosts and sunshine.

The palace, that floats on the ocean, would be a prey to barnacles, to winds and waves, to shoals and rocks, and would soon disappear, without the constant hand of intelligent vital energy to direct and preserve it. Houses untenanted and uncared for soon decay. Leaks unstopped, broken windows unrepaired, and vermin unrestrained, soon make them unfit for habitation. Farms and plantations go back speedily to weeds and wilderness when uncultivated. Great cities like Babylon and Nineveh are soon so covered with dust that we have to dig to find their ruins.

Decay is written over every form of man-made wealth. There is needed constantly the touch of the laborer for its preservation.

Gold, silver and precious stones are the least subject to decay. They are not, however, made, but found, and simply refined and polished. The indestructibility of silver and gold have made them the money metals of the world, quite as much as their rarity, their beauty and malleability. In them wealth could be stored and moth and rust would not corrupt.

But even gold and silver will disappear. The thief will break through and steal. They must be, therefore, carefully guarded. The tax or levy of the government for its part in the protection must be met, so that even gold and silver must also gradually slip away.

Decay is upon all wealth and the hand of the laborer must be ever present for its preservation.

This law is universal. Even the Divine Creator must continue to uphold his creation. His sustaining hand cannot be withdrawn. He must preserve by his power and ever guide and direct, or disorder and chaos will ensue.

Usury or interest presumes to ignore this order of nature and demands not only that the borrower shall resist this tendency of capital to decay, but shall also pay a price for the privilege.

That any one should undertake to care for and preserve the property of another without compensation is unreasonable, but that any one should voluntarily pay a premium for the privilege can only be explained by misguided judgment or a perverted moral sense.

No one would be responsible for, and care for and pay tax upon the money of another and himself get from it no return. Trustees and administrators receive, and feel they earn, a commission for this caring for the property of others.

When this wealth is in the form of a tool, or manufacturing plant, the responsibility is greater. The owner asks that it be preserved perfectly. There must be no decline in value, from new improved machinery, and all accidents must be made good; if destroyed by fire, it must be rebuilt. To take this for a year or term of years, is a responsibility no one would feel justified in assuming in justice to himself. He would be using his own vital force to preserve the perishable property of another.

A man has a farm, fertile and well improved, and well stocked. He is to be absent for a time. He asks as a favor that another watch it with care, preserve the stock in condition, if any die, replace them, and in short, so preserve that he shall have the farm at his return, just as fertile, the stock just as young and valuable, the implements unworn and no signs of decay on the buildings; if any burn, rebuild them. This would be a favor only the kindest and weakest of neighbors or friends would undertake, and what no man would be justified in asking of another. This is loaning without interest and this is the borrower, who pays only the principal and no increase.

The usurer says, Care for my property and pay me for the opportunity. Keep it intact. Make good every loss and return to me an increase which you by your energy and effort may produce.

The rates of interest greatly vary. The average in the United States is about seven per cent., by statistics of the government only recently issued. At seven per cent., interest paid annually or added to debt for ten years, the debt is doubled.

The usurer or interest taker says, You take this hundred dollars and care for it for me for ten years and then bring me two hundred dollars. Take this wheat and this corn and in ten years bring me back just twice the amount. Take these horses and these sheep and cattle and care for them for ten years and return them just as good as they are now, and other horses, cattle and sheep in equal number, which you have produced in these ten years.

Take this shop with all its tools and implements and care for it so that in ten years you can return it to me in as perfect order as now, and also build me with your labor and energy another shop, just like it, and equip it in every way just as complete as this, and on my return give both to me. Take this farm, fertile as it is, with its buildings and animals and implements, and preserve them perfectly, not a thing shall decay or decline in value; make good every loss, and at the end of ten years return it to me and also another farm which you have earned during these ten years, of equal acreage and fertility, equally improved with live stock and implements.

The usurer gains the preservation of his own perishable property, and he gains also the product of the vital force of his victim.

This law of decay is a natural limitation to the accumulation of any producer. As decay begins at once, a part of the vital energy must be expended in the preservation of that already produced. As the accumulations increase, more energy is required for its preservation, and less remains for active production. Time does not relax his work of ruin, and the resisting energy must be constant. The tendency to decay is such that soon the energy required to preserve that already gained leaves none to produce, and the accumulations must cease.

To this point the rich fool in the parable had come. He had abundance accumulated and the problem was to preserve it, until he could consume it. "This will I do, I will pull down my barns, and build greater; and there will I bestow all my fruits and my goods. And I will say to my soul, Soul, thou hast much goods laid up for many years; take thine ease, eat, drink, and be merry."

The usurer hands his goods to another to build the barns and keep for him, while he is free from its care; and, more, he requires of his victim not only that he shall preserve, resisting all decay, but that he shall actually pay him for the privilege.

Had the rich fool not lived in his day, when usury was a crime, but in this age of folly, he would have apportioned his goods among his foolisher neighbors upon interest, to keep for him, and then not only he, for "many years," but his posterity forever, could be at ease, eating, drinking, and making merry. The silly borrowers would supply all the needs of his endowed family, for the privilege of caring for the goods.

CHAPTER XXII

THE DEBT HABIT

The debt habit of mind is the disposition or tendency to look to things we have not as necessary to our success: To yearn for other opportunities and other means than those we have in our hands: To feel helpless without them and willing to incur debt to secure them. The independent, self-reliant disposition takes account of its own powers and opportunities and means, and plans with these to accomplish the very most. This old self-reliant, independent spirit, that scorned debt, has largely passed away. To incur debt is now the common habit and has become respectable.

All evil-doers encourage and stimulate the particular fashion or habit or appetite or passion on which they thrive. Usury thrives on debt. If no one was in debt then usurers would be harmless. It is this debt habit that gives them the large field for their operations and secures to them their harvest.

The agreement to pay interest preserves for a time the feeling of independence that would be wounded by receiving a loan as a favor. There is usually a feeling of joy and elation in the borrower that confidence in him is so great, and his credit is so high, that he can be entrusted with a loan.

By incurring a debt there seems to promise the opening up of opportunities that have been denied, and a possible field for the successful exertion of his pent up energies.

The present intended use of the loan, too, seems so attractive and profitable, and the buoyant, hopeful spirit does not doubt that the loan can be easily and promptly repaid.

The temptations to debt do not come to the vicious and idle and worthless, but to the most worthy, industrious, talented, reliable and enterprising, those who will be the most productive in their fields of effort. Its very approach is flattering and therefore so hard to resist.

A bright, intelligent, noble young man with high aims and worthy purposes yearns for an education, but the opportunities seem to be denied him; but there is a fund at low interest at his service.

A lively, energetic young man, with industrious and economical habits, is anxious to engage in business; his youth, character and energy bring the loan to his feet.

The young man with pure yearning for domestic life and a home, with a reputation that is above reproach and of commendable energy and thrift, has a home pressed upon him, to be paid for in long-time payments. He can fill it with furniture "on the installment plan." With intellectual taste, he can fill his library with just the books he desires "on the installment plan." Is he musical in his taste, he can fill his parlor with musical instruments "on the installment plan." His needs and tastes can all be gratified at once by incurring debt. To avoid debt there must be a determined and unremitted effort to resist. Few have been able to escape. The aggregate of private indebtedness can not be told.

Few manufacturing plants are free from debt. They are usually carrying all the load their credit enables them to secure. Railroads and other corporations are under bonded debts that tax their trade to the utmost to sustain.

Counties and municipalities have caught the contagious habit. Bonds are issued to build school houses, town halls, viaducts, water-works, and pave streets.

There lies on this table a list of all the cities in this great land, the United States, with their number of inhabitants and their bonded debts. There are but six small cities in the long list without debt. In some the amount is enormous, the city debt in cases running up to one hundred and one hundred and fifty, and two hundred dollars per inhabitant. That is, there is a city debt on each man, woman and child of two hundred dollars. On this amount interest must be paid, twelve dollars per year, one dollar per month for every man, woman and child.

There lies also on the table a report of the financial condition of the nearest great city. It is rendered in a cheerful mood and declares the city's credit "tip top." The indebtedness is eight millions, but the assessed valuation of the city is so high that two million more bonds can be issued before the limit of indebtedness is reached as established by the general law. This is regarded as a most favorable showing and the assurance is given that all the contemplated public improvements can be pushed without interruption. There is no thought of stopping until the extreme limit is reached.

This habit extends to the churches and benevolent enterprises. There is scarcely a church that is not paying interest on some debt. Local societies are often greatly hindered in their work. A benevolent agency of one of the largest and richest denominations issued a piteous appeal to their constituents for help, declaring that the interest on their debts amounted to one thousand dollars per week.

The debt habit has seized the nations and the most enlightened. This is so true that debts are, in pleasantry, spoken of as a sign of a nation's progress. These aggregate billions are rapidly increasing.

The Chancellor of the Exchequer says the debt of England was reduced five hundred millions in twenty years. To the astonishment of all the world, the United States began to pay her debt, eighteen hundred million, in thirty years. But these stand alone among the nations. The national debts do not grow less, but are rapidly increasing. Both the United States and England are now increasing their indebtedness each year.

The world has gone debt mad. It has become a great harvest field, ripe for the usurers.

Debts may at times be unavoidable. They may at times be positively beneficial. There may be times when the system is in such a condition that it is necessary to take arsenic in small doses, but arsenic has no place in the menu of a healthy man. So debts may be necessary to those who have fallen into decay or have been unfortunate, but they should find no place in the normally healthy financial conditions of an individual or incorporation or nation.

Debts make no man the richer. A man is no richer when he has secured a loan, than he was before. Paying debts makes no man poorer. He but relieves himself of the property of another.

Paying a national debt destroys no wealth. If owed at home, it is but a transfer from one hand or pocket to another.

Adjusting the world's debts, private, corporate, municipal, or national, the world would remain as rich and productive. Not a material thing would perish. No man would suffer the loss of any right or of any property, but it would be the destruction of the device by which the usurers appropriate to themselves the productions of others.

Freed from this debt habit of mind, and the independent, self-reliant disposition replaced, this anomalous condition would disappear; the producer would receive again his full earnings and the great army of parasites, that has grown up, and that feed so richly on the labors of others, would be compelled to turn producers or perish.

CHAPTER XXIII

THE BORROWER IS SERVANT TO THE LENDER

Solomon's declaration that, "The borrower is servant to the lender," was spoken without reference to usury. Loaning upon increase was not lawful in his day, and was condemned by him in his proverb, "He that by usury and unjust gain increaseth his substance, he shall gather it for him that will have pity on the poor."

A loan binds the borrower to the lender though he pay no increase. There comes a sense of subserviency and subordination that can not be thrown off.

He becomes steward of another's goods, and frees the owner of their care, but they remain subject to the owner's order. The preservation of goods hinder any great accumulation by any single producer, but if he can be freed from its care, then all his energies can be used to continue production. Many find it as hard to keep property as it is to earn it.

The hunter or fisherman takes with him his lackey to carry his game. If game is plentiful and the hunter successful, he would, otherwise, soon be compelled to discontinue his hunt from the burden of fish and game. But, freed from that care and burden, he can continue his hunt indefinitely. So, the borrower, even when he pays no interest, as a lackey, without wages, cares for the earnings of the lender, leaving him free to continue his earning unhindered.

A valet cares for the clothes of his master until he calls for them. The borrower, without interest, as a valet, without pay, cares for the goods of the lender until he needs them.

The independent spirit of the borrower is not immediately lost. The servile spirit and conscious sense of bondage may not be felt at once. Likely the first sensation on receiving a loan is an elation bordering on ecstasy.

The poor man who is offered a loan is usually greatly delighted. There is hope of relief from the limitations and restraints that have been as a wall round about him. The loan seems to throw down these walls and give him an opportunity to secure greater results and achieve success. But the delight is transient and the sense of greater liberty is brief. The prison walls are down, but the debt holds him like a ball and chain. He has only exchanged one restraint for another worse; he has leaped from the pan into the fire. The spirit loses its hopefulness and independence and becomes servile and cringing.

Milton represents our first parents, after their first sin, as intoxicated in delight, but the consciousness of their degradation and shame soon followed. So the first sensation from a loan is of relief and hope; the future looks bright, but the sense of subjection to the lender is sure to follow.

He forfeits the free, independent, self-reliant spirit that scorns dependence upon any man. He only looks the whole world in the face, who owes no man a cent.

CHAPTER XXIV

USURY ENSLAVES THE BORROWER

Timon of Athens said, "No usurer, but has a fool for a slave."

The borrower without usury loses his free and independent spirit and becomes cringing and servile, but when interest is paid it increases the severity of the servile service.

The lackey must not only care for the game taken, but he must add to the bag from his own hunting. He not only cares for the fish his master caught but must add to the basket from his own catching. The valet must not only perfectly preserve the clothes of his master, but must add to his wardrobe.

The borrower of the usurer must protect and preserve every farthing in value of the property or goods, and must also increase the amount.

The estimate put upon the mental condition of the person who will submit to such an imposition, by "Timon of Athens," must be admitted as fairly just, for a heathen. From the almost universal practice of usury, and the vast numbers enslaved, we must also admit that Solomon, the wisest man that ever lived, knew what he was saying, when he slyly called us all fools in his proverb, "A wise man's heart is at his right hand but a fool's heart is at his left."

The object of the usurer in making a loan is to secure the service of the borrower; it may be called a favor, an opportunity, an accommodation, but that is its purpose and its effect. It may be called capital or a tool for production, but the appropriation of the service of the borrower is the result sought and secured.

To secure the service of a horse, there must be an outgo of wealth in its purchase price and in its harness and the vehicle. The service received is the return, the compensation for the payment made. That is money invested and repaid in service. The price was in accordance with the service the animal would be able to render. For more and better service a higher price must be paid.

There must be an expenditure to secure the service of a chattel slave. The purchase price must be paid and the tools and material or plantation must be supplied before his services are available. The price paid is in accordance with a reasonable estimate of the service the slave will be able to render during life. The outlay is made in consideration of an equivalent in service.

A loan is made for the same purpose and secures the same result. The price of the horse or slave must be paid before the service can be claimed. The loan must be made before there can be a pretext of a claim upon the services of the borrower.

There is this difference, however, that the purchaser pays for the services he expects to receive; he makes a real outlay for what is to be given him. The usurer pays nothing, he does not give a farthing; he makes no outlay; he merely changes the deposit from the bank vault, or his strong box, to his victim, and requires from him such an ample security that it is as safe in his hands as remaining in the vault. That he has bought the service of the borrower as another bought the service of the horse or chattel slave is untrue. He has given no equivalent. He retains every farthing of his wealth safely deposited with his victim. The service he receives does not diminish the value of his property nor discharge any portion of his claim.

The usurer, like all those who appropriate the labors of their slaves, claims that he is a real benefit to his borrower. He has given him an opportunity of advancement that he could not otherwise have had. He points to him possibly with some degree of pride, especially if he seems greatly prospered. The owner of colored slaves pointed to his well-fed and well-clothed and happy people, merry in their cabins, and made a claim that was equally plausible; that these people are far better off and far happier than they could be in freedom.

Their well-kept, happy, care-free condition did not make them freemen. They were slaves, though they may have been happy. They were slaves, though they preferred bondage to being their own masters. The usurer's prosperous victim is not therefore a freeman. Though he should prefer debt to independence, that does not make him free.

No one prefers to be in debt. Debts are chosen as the least of the evils. The natural resources are occupied and the opportunities of life are denied. Lands and all tools of production are withheld and the horns of the dilemma are debt or privation. The independent spirit shrinks from debt until the struggle of life becomes desperate, when he turns to the other evil and is enslaved.

This is not a temptation that comes to the idle and vicious. They could not secure a loan though they tried. An indolent, dissipated and vicious chattel slave would not find a purchaser in the market.

It is the industrious, virtuous and economical young man that is of value to the usurer, and the better his character, the greater his worth. For this reason their virtues are cried up to the usurers, as the favorable qualities of the chattel were presented in the slave marts. To secure a loan is an evidence of confidence in his business ability, and an evidence of the appreciation of his character. It is a flattering compliment, and promising relief to a condition that seems hopeless, he permits the yoke of bondage to be fastened upon him.

The usurer's slave is cheaper than the chattel. It requires less wealth to secure an equal amount of service. A loan of five thousand dollars at the prevailing rate of seven per cent. will bring to the usurer more than one dollar, clear gain, for every working day. That is as much as any one man, not professional or specially skilled, can hope to produce with that amount of capital, after caring for himself and his home. The borrower secures the lender from all loss, he largely relieves him from oversight, he directs his own labors, supports himself wholly; if sick, he supplies a substitute that the service does not stop, and when from the infirmities of age he is no longer able to give the required amount of service, one dollar per day, he returns the loan in full, which may be bound upon another victim, and thus continued forever.

In the days of chattel slavery labor was not so cheap. The price of a strong, faithful young colored slave, and the value of the tools for him to use, and the proportionate part of the plantation necessary for him to work, was about equal to the above loan. Then he must be clothed and fed; his work must be directed; if sick his labor was lost, and he must receive medical and other care; all risks of harvest from drouth or flood must be incurred by the owner, and the slave's term of service was limited by his death, when his purchase cost was lost, and there must be an outlay by a new purchase. One chattel slave could not bring his master such enormous returns.

Not only does financial slavery exact more labor for the amount invested, but it is more heartless than chattel bondage. The master had a personal interest in the slave he bought. His health and strength was an object of his care and his death a great loss. There was also often a mutual affection developed, as is sometimes found between a man and his horse or affectionate dog. There was sometimes real unfeigned mutual love. The master had a tender care over his slaves in their sicknesses and in their decrepit age, and sorrowed at their graves. The slaves were inconsolable in their grief at the death of their master.

The usurer has no personal interest in his slave. He has no care for his health or his life; they are of no interest to him. He may live in a distant state and has no anxiety about those who serve him. Their personal ills give him no concern. When they die, there is no loss nor any additional outlay required; the bonds are simply transferred to others, and the service is not interrupted.

Many faithful, industrial and honest borrowers are unable to return the loan. It is as difficult to retain property as it is to earn it. New inventions, new processes, new methods, new legislation and the changing fashions and customs, often sweep property from the shrewd and careful. "Riches make themselves wings; they fly away." If for any cause the borrower fails there is scant sympathy from the usurer. He charges him with being deficient in business management and thriftless. If the yoke of bondage galls and becomes so painful that in his distress the debtor turns from the struggle in one direction to struggle in another in hope of relief, he calls him fickle; and if at last, after a long and hard service, he is unable to return the loan in full, he calls him dishonest. His ear is deaf to the voice, "Is not this the fast that I have chosen? to loose the bands of wickedness, to undo the heavy burdens, and to let the oppressed go free."

There are those in debt yet struggling against hope to be free. They are slaving at work, but making no progress toward relief. The crisis must come. In the race with biting usury that knows no rest, night nor day, year in and year out, that knows no sickness nor delay, that keeps step with time, there is but one possible result. There can be but one final result, though the debtor may have a start far in advance, but if in the race it has become neck and neck, the end is near. Usury will sweep on with full wind, and unslacking pace, when the debtor falls exhausted. There is comfort, however, though the race be lost, for the distress of poverty is less than the agony of hopeless debt.

The old and ruined, who have lived honorable and industrious lives, who have endeavored to do their part in all the relations of life, yet have been in the slavery of debt all their days, and when their powers began to fail were stripped of the earnings of years, and besides, are compelled to bear the name of dishonorable debtors, are the most worthy of sympathy of any the world knows. The decrepit old chattel slave had hope of a home until the end, and a decent burial, but the debtor has nothing, not even an honorable name.

The young, who are yet free from personal debt, should be warned, and should not permit themselves to be beguiled by any of the allurements held out, nor by flatteries. As one prizes his independent spirit and freedom from the dictation of others, as he desires a successful life and a peaceful old age, he should avoid debt. As a Christian, who desires unrestrained Christian fellowship, whose benevolence will be from the kindness and love of his own heart, as one who wishes to bless all he meets, and to leave a name associated only with hallowed memories, he should avoid debt.

"Owe no man anything, but love one another."

CHAPTER XXV

USURY OPPRESSES THE POOR

Moses, Solomon and the prophets connect usury with the oppression of the poor. For this reason many have thought the divine prohibition of usury applied only to loans to the poor. By careful attention we will find that its evils are not confined to the immediate participants in the transaction. In the natural operation of economic laws the ultimate burden rests upon the poor. It is clear that when each member of a community contributes his portion to the common welfare the burdens are equally distributed. When any one fails to contribute his proportion the burdens are made heavier for the other members, and the burdens increase as the number increases of those who for any cause fail to contribute their part.

This is true in the family home life. When every member of the household is able, and with cheerful willingness does his full part for the family support and comfort, the burden is equally distributed. Let one member of the family be in any way disabled and his duties must be performed by others. If several are disabled the burdens upon the others may be greatly increased. If any are indolent the burdens are made heavy upon those who are industrious.

The same is true in the larger family, the community and the state, for political economy is but enlarged home economy. The burdens are lightest when every one contributes his full share to the general welfare. When any are idle the duties become heavier upon those who are faithful.

Usury makes it possible for many to live upon incomes from their property. They are not classed, nor do they class themselves, among those who are personally productive. This makes it necessary for the poor, those who have no property, to produce more in order to house and clothe and feed the community.

But those non-productive persons are consumers and are the most active consumers. They make heavy drafts upon the energies of others. They become extravagant in their habits and the spendthrifts of the world; while in proportion to their extravagant habits there must be severity and simplicity in the habits of the industrious and productive, on whom the support of the community rests.

The world does not grow richer nor are the conditions of life for one class eased by the extravagance of another class.

It is sometimes said that the idleness and the wasteful habits of some are for the benefit of others because they make a demand for more work. It would give the lumberman and nail-cutter and carpenter and glazier and plasterer and painter more work to call back the fire department and let the house burn, but that is not the way to house the houseless. Extravagance is wasteful destruction of property.

"It is insisted upon both moral and economic grounds that no public benefit of any kind arises from the existence of a rich idle class. Their incomes must be paid, though inconsistent with the public good. To illustrate, the London and Southwestern railroad contemplated a reduction of fares in cars of the third-class. It was defeated because it might reduce the dividends. The poor could not be relieved lest it should reduce the incomes of the idle."—Ruskin.

That family is happy and prosperous in which every member contributes personally his portion to its support and comfort. That condition affords the highest measure of relief for all. It is unfortunate if there should be an idler in the home who, as a parasite, feeds on the industry of the others; it is a double misfortune if that idler proves a spendthrift to waste the thrifty gatherings of the diligent. The same economic principles make it necessary for the highest good of every individual in the community that each shall contribute his personal part. "If any will not work neither shall he eat." If any insist upon eating and yet will not work, it imposes an oppressive burden on others to compel them to supply his table.

Again: The limiting of production is a hardness to the poor. Their welfare requires the largest possible product along every line of human needs. Over-production is a term of the trade and means only that the supply has become so great that it cannot be sold at prices satisfactory to the trade. But as the prices fall the market broadens. Consumption increases with the increasing abundance, and that which it was not possible for certain classes to enjoy now comes within their reach and may become possible to even the poorest. There never can be an over-supply of fruits and vegetables and grains and meats and shoes and clothes and salt and oil and fuel and houses until the wants of the poorest are supplied. Their welfare requires that there shall be no restraining of the supply until they come out of their huts into houses; until they can shed their rags and dress in clothes both comfortable and attractive; until their tables are supplied with nutritious food; until they have the means of discovering and cultivating their æsthetic nature by shaking off the repellant conditions in which they are mostly compelled to live.

The practice of usury restrains the supply by freeing so large a part of the people from the necessity of active productive effort by the incomes from their properties. Many born to wealth have never felt the necessity, and have never made an effort nor turned a thought along productive lines. The world has lost all that they might have added to the world's supply for human needs. Many, who have been successful in accumulation early in life, retire from active work while yet in full vigor, because they are relieved of the necessity by the income of usury or increase, and the most valuable portion of their lives is lost to the world.

Production is further limited by the demand that it shall yield an increase on the property employed. The shop is shut down when the goods cannot be sold at such a price as to pay a satisfactory profit on the investment. The shop stands idle until the stock is depleted and the demand raises the price of the goods and then the shop is again opened. The workmen could go on with their work, supplying the world with their goods, bringing the price down until within the reach of the poorest, but it is the owner of the shop that holds the key and demands that the supply shall be so far restrained that the price shall yield a satisfactory increase on the property.

Inventions and improved tools are a blessing to the poor when they make labor so productive that they can enjoy results of labor that could not be enjoyed by them before. They are not a blessing when used to gain an increase on wealth by employing less labor. Their proper use is to make labor more productive; their perverted use is to make property more profitable.

There is a natural restraint by the law of supply and demand when all needs are so supplied that there is no longer a sufficient compensation to the producer; but it is a perverted and unrighteous restraint to place property between productive labor and human needs and demand a reward for it before these human needs shall be satisfied. There is an utter want of pity for the poor in permitting them to go unhoused, unfed and unclothed, unless there shall be a profit by increase in supplying their wants. True benevolence requires that labor shall be made so effective as to fill every human need, but pure selfishness uses property to supply the need for a gain. This restraint for an increase on property is oppression of the poor for a price.

CHAPTER XXVI

USURY OPPRESSES THE POOR—

CONTINUED

The influence of any act is not limited to the person acting. The righteous act of a righteous man blesses himself and his generation and generations yet unborn. So the influence of a wrong act is not limited to the wrong-doer, but extends to others and is harmful to those who had no voluntary part in the act. Though the wrong be a personal habit and the sinner be himself the greatest sufferer, yet it is impossible to avoid causing distress to others who are themselves innocent.

Equity between those who participate in a wrong does not make a wrong act righteous. Thieves may be just among themselves, in the division of the spoils secured from others, but that does not make them upright men, nor does it make their business honest. If it were possible to preserve equity between the borrower and the lender upon usury, yet that would not justify the act nor remove the evil. The collection of their profits, which they divide equitably among themselves, imposes a burden upon others who have no part in the transaction. Their satisfactory agreement does not make the transaction less detrimental to the general good. It may the rather partake of the nature of a conspiracy against the public welfare.

The promoter of an enterprise on borrowed capital is practically but the agent of the lender. He may be the director and manager but he so conducts his undertaking as to gather the usury from others. When the opportunities for profitable investments become rare, and money accumulates and is lying idle, such promoters with their schemes are encouraged in order to gain a profit on the investment, though others suffer by it.

There lies upon this table a booklet, written in 1841, which charges and proves complicity between the bankers and brokers of New York at that time. The bankers loaned the brokers the money which they reloaned at very high rates. The banks refused accommodations to those in pressing need, compelling them to go to the brokers and to submit to their extortionate demands.

Though there may be an equitable arrangement between the owner of property and his broker and between the broker and his promoter, yet in the last analysis it will be found that this equitable arrangement, in its ultimate result, is of the nature of a conspiracy to compel the innocent poor to pay the profits of both; their consent is not first secured nor do they gain a single advantage and they are helpless to resist.

Though the transaction may have been between the rich, a rich lender and a rich borrower, yet the final result is that the interest is paid by the poor. In Calvin's letter of apology he supposes a case of equity between a rich land owner who is in need of ready money and the man who has money to buy a farm, but instead lends to his rich landlord and takes a mortgage. In this case the tenants of the borrower must pay the interest and finally the principal also. This increases the hardness of their hard lot. Though Calvin seems to appreciate the severe conditions of the ordinary tenant in his day, yet he fails to recognize that the very illustration he gives would result in greater oppression.

When one entrusts his money to a broker for investment he does not come in contact with those who earn the interest. It may pass through a number of agents and the source from which the interest is drawn is not regarded. When one entrusts his money to the "Security Co." in their great building, surrounded by all appearances of unlimited wealth, it is not realized that the interest returned is wrung from the poor. Money does not lie in the vaults. It is loaned to others who as agents do collect or gather from the poor. A loan is made to a milling company and the interest is gathered from all who buy their flour. A loan is made to a landlord and he collects the usury from his tenants. A loan is made to a street car company and increase is collected from the employes and from every rider. A loan is made to a merchant and he collects from his customers.

It is easy to see who pay the interest when we make a common pawnbroker our agent and see in his dingy rooms the evident distress and needs of his callers. Many shrink from his oppressions who are deceived by the splendid surroundings of the "Security Co." But the interest is exacted from the same class as truly by one as by the other.

Usury oppresses the poor by raising the price of all that he consumes. Without being consulted and without the power of resistance he must pay tribute to property for the very necessities of life.

He lives in a rented house. The owner has placed a mortgage on this house and the tenant must pay the interest and more in his rental or be ejected. The bread he must have is from wheat raised on mortgaged land and the interest must be met in the price of wheat. The mill is mortgaged in which it is ground and the interest must be paid in the increased price of flour. The railroad is bonded and the interest on the bonds must be paid in the price of its transportation, and the merchant has a loan to enable him to do business and the interest on this loan must be met in the increase of the profits on flour and all other goods he handles. By usury a tribute is levied on his bread from the wheat in the field until it reaches his tables.

In the same way he pays interest in the price of his meat, which is raised on a mortgaged farm, transported over a bonded railroad, dressed in a mortgaged abattoir and sold by a dealer doing business on borrowed capital.

The same is true of his clothes; a first tribute must be paid to property by the raw cotton or wool, then the transportation and the factory and the merchant, in addition to the compensation for their services, must meet also the interest upon their loans, and the whole is summed up in the price the poor man must pay. He has no option in the matter; he has no alternative, no method by which he can escape. The same is true with regard to his fuel and his light.

The same is true with regard to car fares. In every ride he pays an enormous tribute to invested wealth. The writer made a careful estimate of the accounts of a car line in a small city where the number of riders bore small comparison with the crowded cars of any metropolis. When the cost of maintenance of the plant, including the wear and tear and all repairs, and the cost of operation, covering all current expenses, including taxes, were compared with the receipts from the patrons of the road, it was found that less than two cents per passenger was necessary to pay these charges and that three cents had gone to pay the interest on the enormous bonded indebtedness and dividends on the inflated stock.

The wage-earner, the pensioner and every person living upon an annuity or fixed income from any source, must thus pay usury or interest on obligations they never incurred. A large portion of their living is thus taken from them, and under a system of general usury they have no way of avoiding it. They must pay an enormous tribute to property in providing the common necessaries of life.

Usury lowers the poor man's wages. The owners of property forbid its use until such a concession is made by the laborer as they may demand for the material and tools of production. Those who will use them and give the owner the highest return for their use secure the work, *i.e.*, those who will bid the labor the lowest, who will use the tools and work up the material the cheapest.

The demand of capital has come to absorb a large portion of the produce of labor. In 1890 the wage-earners created a value of $3,579,168,172 and received out of it wages amounting to $1,981,228,321, leaving in the hands of the employers $1,687,939,851. Labor thus received a little less than 53 per cent. of its product. In 1900 the wage-earners created a value of $4,640,784,931 and received out of it wages amounting to $2,323,407,257, leaving in the hands of employers $2,317,377,674. The employers and employes divided labor's product so evenly that the difference does not amount to one-eighth of one per cent.

The decade 1890 to 1900 has been of unprecedented prosperity to capital, but the advantages to labor have not appeared. When the number of laborers at the beginning and the close of the decade are considered the annual income of the wage-earner at the close of the decade is actually $7 per year less than ten years ago.

The tribute to property must first be gained, the wages are secondary. If the tribute is not paid the enterprise is regarded as not successful and the industry closes.

There is no protection for the laborer except the selfishness of capitalists themselves in competition to secure the services of labor. But the selfish strife has rather resulted in the combination of their capital to dispense with labor or to cause the same labor to produce more by the employment of more capital. The effect is to give employment to capital rather than to labor. If labor can be dispensed with by borrowing more capital, then a loan is secured and the laborer is dismissed. Thus capital is made to crowd out the laborer and gains for itself his reward. This diminishes the call for labor and increases the number of the unemployed and they become competitors for the privilege of working. The opportunities for labor becoming fewer, the strife for work becomes fiercer. The laborer is helpless to resist, as his wants do not stop; his family must be fed and clothed and housed. The struggle is unequal between "flesh and blood" and a material thing that, by a false economy, is given not only the power of self-support but also continuous increase. For this reason combinations of laborers never have been and never can be successful in a conflict with capital. So long as the false principle is admitted, all efforts must fail. So long as it is granted that property has earning power, the effort will be made by the owners of property, and always successfully made, to have property receive the larger portion of the reward. The true order will be reversed; the laborer will be given a mere subsistence while the increase will be claimed for the capital; the very opposite of the true order, the mere preservation or subsistence of the capital, while all the increase belongs to the laborers.

CHAPTER XXVII

USURY OPPRESSES THE POOR—

CONTINUED

Usury makes it possible to impose on the poor the principal burden of taxation. Though taxes are levied upon property it is a delusion to think that those who own no property pay no taxes. By usury the taxes are easily slipped upon the poor.

If the tax levy is one per cent. on property then in a year the one hundred dollars has been decreased by one dollar and is but ninety-nine, unless that dollar has been supplied from other earnings of the owner. Thus vacant lots, jewels and hoarded stores are a burden to their owner. But when the property can add to itself an increase, then there need be no diminution of the amount, and no sacrifice is necessary on the part of the owner. If the wealth is placed in the form of a loan on mortgage on a house, the tenant in his rental pays the interest on that mortgage, which meets the tax and also yields a revenue to the owner, and leaves the wealth undiminished. The tenant earned the tax, and both property and owner are relieved. The mortgage may be upon a manufacturing plant, when the operatives pay the tax from their earnings.

The bonded debt of a city or state, in the ultimate result, is collected from the productive labor. To pay the interest and principal of the bonded debt of a city the tax levy is increased, and a greater proportionate amount of labor is appropriated.

Laboring people without property are often amazed at the indifference of property holders when a great bonded debt is incurred, as both interest and principal are to be paid by a tax upon property. Those who make the loan to the city, and all who hold mortgages and dividend paying properties, are complacent because the taxes of a hundred years would never diminish their property a dollar, though the tax levy should be doubled. It would raise the interest on money, diminish the price of labor and raise the price of goods, but those who profit by the gain of usury are untouched by it.

Recently complaints were made by the tenants of one of the poor districts of London because their rentals had been greatly increased. The reply of the landlord was direct and clear: "You have voted for public improvements and now you must pay for them."

The same is true of the interest and principal of the national debt. The revenue is raised from a levy upon importations, as, for example, tea, the tax on which is ten cents per pound. The tax is collected from the importer and by him attached to the price for which it is sold to the wholesale dealer and by him attached to the price he charges the retail dealer and by him the amount is collected from the consumer. Sufficient notice is usually given that the importer and the dealers may dispose of all their goods before the tariff is removed. A public announcement of such a purpose was recently made in reference to the tax upon tea.

The tax collected from the consumer is far heavier than the mere levy of the government. The importer demands a profit on the amount of revenue tax he has paid as well as on the amount he pays for the goods. This results in greatly increasing the burdens of the poor. The revenue tax recently imposed by Great Britain of three pence per cwt. on wheat and five pence per cwt. on flour resulted immediately in the addition of one penny to the price of the four-pound loaf to the consumers.

Again: This attributing to property the quality of self-perpetuation and increase has led to its incorporation and in a manner separation from those who own it. Property must always have an owner.

Personality must always come in else there are no rights to be considered. Labor apart from a person laboring and property apart from a person owning are impersonal and no ethical or moral laws can be applied to them. They are only physical forces and material things. The wind may push against a tree and overcome its resistance and the tree falls. That is merely an abstract force against a material thing. But when my energy is exerted against your tree and destroys it, then personal responsibility and personal rights must be considered. A righteous adjustment between labor and capital can never be arrived at without the consideration of the personal elements on both sides. The moral and ethical laws must be applied as well as the physical and economic.

Incorporated property, however, has eliminated from it the ethical and moral responsibility of personality and is regarded as possessed only of economic and physical qualities and restrained only by legal statutes.

Incorporated properties are not generally managed by those who own them. The managers are employed by the owners, who are ready to pay large compensation to those who have the tact and brain and nerve power and peculiar quality of conscience to gain for them a satisfactory increase. It is their work to press this irresponsible material body up against "flesh and blood."

The incorporation employs the laborer when his labor earns a satisfactory dividend on the capital, and lays him off or discharges him whenever it seems most to the advantage of the investment. A plant is built and operated for a time and then the plant is closed, or the location is changed without the slightest regard to the sacrifices of the poor laborers who have gathered around and are left stranded.

Laborers everywhere throughout Christendom need and beg for a Sabbath of rest, but neither physical needs nor conscientious scruples are regarded when a greater dividend can be gained in seven days than in six.

On the part of the workman, resistance is useless. He can do nothing but yield to the economic and physical force managed by those in whom human sympathy and pity for the suffering and helpless are not permitted. The dividend must be gained though it be necessary to grind the poor.

The owner of this steel plant is in a distant city. All employes, from the manager down to the porter, must so serve that he shall receive the dividend. This mercantile house is owned by a woman on a pleasure trip round the world. All who are connected with this business must so serve and sacrifice that she shall receive her income regularly. This railroad is owned by those who have gone a-yachting in southern seas. It must be so managed that the revenues shall not fail whatever the sacrifice required of others.

The writer once heard an American statesman, who afterward became President of the United States, deliver an elaborate and carefully prepared oration on a great occasion, in which he discussed the growing power and controlling influence in state and national affairs of incorporations. He did not formulate a remedy but said, "The problem to be solved by the next generation is, how shall the people be protected against the encroachments of incorporated wealth?" It need scarcely be said that there was no discussion of that question during the campaign which closed with his election to the presidency.

Usury is both the basis of the incorporation and the instrument of its oppression. Incorporated wealth must not be permitted to claim personal rights and yet escape personal responsibility. It must be held to the same ethical and moral laws as the individual. Personal responsibility must not be eliminated from property. It must not be divested of personal responsibility and then pressed as a mere material thing up against "flesh and blood."

No instrument of oppression ever surpassed in severity the usury of incorporated wealth and retained the pretense of respectability. It is sucking the blood of the poor every hour, yet they cherish and pet the vampire, not realizing that it is their blood upon which it feeds.

CALVIN ELLIOTT

CHAPTER XXVIII

USURY OPPRESSES THE POOR—
CONCLUDED

Usury increases its burdens in proportion to the poverty. It is the most oppressive upon the poorest. Property in any measure is a relief. However small the amount may be, to that degree it assists in bearing the burden. Those who have a home are relieved of the burden of usury by rent. Those who own their shops or farms on which they can employ their labor are relieved of the usury of tools and material. From the conditions now prevailing the burden of usury rests on all those, the half of whose income is the product of their own labor. The one who receives one-half his income from the interest on property and one-half from his own labor has no advantage from usury. The income of his labor would bring him as many of the comforts of life as his labor now does, plus the income from his property. There is no advantage until a greater part of the income is derived from property. A small savings account, adding a few dollars annually to the income, is a very small offset to the constant drain from usury in all that we buy and upon all our earnings. The full burden however is upon those who have nothing but their own productive energy; who receive only wages and must buy in the market. As the relief afforded by property decreases, the oppressive burden of usury in present conditions increases.

It is a fair estimate that usury is oppressive until relieved by the income from property to the amount of one-half of the entire income received. When less, the oppression begins and leans its full weight and without pity upon the poorest and most helpless.

He that has no property is dependent upon others for employment and in his wages must give a part of his product as tribute to the capital he uses. This, in the case of the average wage earner in this country, is not less than one-third, that is, he who earns one dollar and a half will receive as wages one dollar, the other half dollar is retained by the employer as due for the capital invested. Then having no home he must pay tribute to property in shelter for himself and family. The rent will be higher in proportion to the poverty of the apartments. The poorest tenement returns the highest rate of interest to the landlord.

His decreased wages do not make the necessities of life proportionately cheap to him. He pays usury in the price of the fuel which he burns, of the oil, gas or electric light in his home. In the price of vegetables, bread and clothes and shoes. There is an increased outgo at every turn which he cannot avoid. He is helpless to resist.

He can but struggle staggering along while work is given and his health and strength remain. When these fail he falls and must become entangled in debt, from which there is no hope of being able to extricate himself.

The state recognizes the hopelessness of the poor man who is in debt and has provided a relief by bankruptcy, by which he may again arise and struggle on. This discharge in bankruptcy is an act of mercy but the relief from the oppressions of usury would be an act of justice. Grinding the helpless poor between low wages and high prices and then relieving them by the act of bankruptcy is only pulling them out of the mill to throw them into the hopper again, for the wage earner who has no protection from any property is between these upper and nether mill stones.

Those who defend the fraud of usury always take to cover behind the widow and the fatherless. They plausibly pretend to be zealous for their protection while endeavoring to hide their own greed. Their pleas are often touchingly pathetic. "A thrifty loving father was taken away by death from a dear wife and sweet little ones. They had always leaned on his strong arms. He was their joy, their protector and their support. This widow and her fatherless children are left with nothing to support them except the saved hard earnings of this husband's life. As these earnings are their only support they are deposited with care with the 'Security Co.' for safety and that the regular interest dues may be received without fail. If there should be one failure they would suffer. The 'Security Co.' loan their deposits as opportunity offers. They take some local mortgages and also some mortgages on western lands. They buy some bonds of a milling trust and also of a railroad and street car line and some national bonds and loan on personal security to local merchants and traders. From all these sources the interest is regularly collected and regularly paid to this widowed mother, without which she and her little fatherless dear ones must suffer. 'Certainly,' they say 'usury is not oppressive to the widow and the fatherless. Usury comes to the help of the helpless.'"

Another faithful industrious father was taken away from his wife and his little ones. He had been their stay and support. He was sober and thrifty but sickness and untoward conditions made accumulations impossible. When he, the head of the home, was taken away there was nothing for the support of these helpless little ones and their widowed mother but her own arms and head and heart. There was no time for sentiment and tears. These little ones must be sheltered and their hungry mouths must be fed. Restraining her grief, she bravely undertakes the heavy task.

She rents a room but the rental is high, for the interest must be paid on a mortgage held by the Security Co. She finally finds a shop where she secures employment but the wages are low, for the shop is heavily mortgaged to the Security Co. and the interest must be paid or the shop will be closed and even this opportunity for scant wages will be lost. The distance requires that she shall ride to her work but the round trip costs two nickels and one of them goes to the Security Co. for interest on their bonds and stock. She buys a loaf of bread but the wheat was raised on a western farm mortgaged to the Security Co. and the interest was charged up against the wheat. The wheat was floured in a trust mill and the interest on the Security Co. bonds were charged up against the flour. It was transported by a railroad that charged up against it the interest on the bonds held by the Security Co. It was baked in a mortgaged oven and handled by a local dealer doing business on capital he had borrowed of the Security Co. How much of her bread money went for interests is an intricate problem. She only notices that her loaf is small.

The same oppressive tribute must be paid on all that she buys to feed and clothe herself and her little ones.

The first widow does not live upon the earnings of her husband. They are untouched at the end of a year nor diminished as the years pass. By the operation of usury she has lived upon the hard earnings of this poor widow. The laborers on the western farms contributed to her support in decreases of wages; the operatives of the railways, the workmen in the mill, the baker and merchant all contribute a portion, but it cannot be denied that the heaviest burden comes upon the poorest. The rich widow has fed her children with the bread which the poor widow earned.

The flaunting sympathy for the poor of those who themselves feed upon them, is rank hypocracy. Nor can those who have grown fat by the practice of usury, condone the crime by tossing back to them a portion of the unjust gain.

"Is it such a fast that I have chosen? A day for a man to afflict his soul?... Is not this the fast that I have chosen?... To undo the heavy burdens and to let the oppressed go free?... Is it not to deal thy bread to the hungry, and that thou bring the poor that are cast out to thy house?"

CALVIN ELLIOTT

CHAPTER XXIX

USURY CENTRALIZES WEALTH

The dictum of Bacon that "Usury gathers the wealth of the realm into few hands" is readily proven and fully verified in the experience of these times. The tendency to centralization under a system of usury or interest-taking is so strong, and the modern result so apparent that the statement only is necessary.

Usury not only enslaves the borrower and oppresses the poor who are innocent of all debt, but it also affects the rich by gathering the wealth of the wealthy into fewer and fewer hands. There is a centralizing draft that threatens and then finally absorbs the smaller fortunes into one colossal financial power. It is as futile to resist this as to resist fate. Wealth cannot be so fortified and guarded as to successfully resist the attack of superior wealth when the practice of usury is permitted. The smaller and weaker fortune, using the same weapon as the larger and stronger, must inevitably be defeated and overcome, and ultimately absorbed.

Rates of interest do not affect the ultimate result. Under a high rate the gathering is rapid, under a low rate the accretions are slower, but the gathering into few hands is none the less sure. Rates of interest only place the convergent center at a nearer or more remote period.

If any interest is right, compound interest is right. When simple interest is due and paid, it may be loaned to another party, and thus the usurer secures interest upon his interest, though not from the same debtor. When the interest is to be paid annually, it is to be assumed, if not paid, that the debtor takes it as a loan in addition to the face of the note of his obligation. This saves the care of receiving and re-loaning to another. The custom of usurers, however, is to renew the note, adding the interest to the face, if unpaid. The mass of bank paper is renewed each ninety days: Compounded four times a year, whether to the same or to another debtor, the result in accretion is the same.

Few realize the rapidity at which a loan increases, accelerating in geometrical progression as time passes. Any loan will double itself at three per cent. in twenty-three and a half years; at seven per cent. in ten and a fourth years, and at ten per cent. in seven and a third years. One dollar loaned for one hundred years, at three per cent., would amount to nineteen dollars; at seven per cent. one thousand dollars, and at ten per cent. thirteen thousand.

The island upon which New York stands was bought from the Indians for the value of twenty-four dollars by Peter Minuits in 1626. Yet, if the purchaser had put his twenty-four dollars at interest, where he could have added it to the principal at the rate of seven per cent., the accumulation would now exceed the total value of the entire city and county of New York.

M. Jennet quotes the elaborate calculation of an ingenious author to show that 100 francs ($20) accumulating at five per cent. compound interest for seven centuries, would be sufficient to buy the whole surface of the globe, both land and water, at the rate of 1,000,000 francs ($200,000) per hectare (nearly four square miles). From this we can gather that $20 at five per cent. compound interest for 700 years, would buy all the earth, mountains, and swamp lands, and water, at $80 per acre.

Another mathematical genius says, had one cent been loaned on the first day of January A.D. 1, interest being allowed at the rate of six per cent. compounded yearly, then 1895 years later—that is on January 1, 1895—the amount due would be $8,497,840,000,000,000,000,000,000,000,000,000,000,000,000,0 00 (8,497,840,000 decillions). If it were desired to pay this in gold, 23.2 grains to the dollar, then taking spheres of pure gold the size of the earth, it would take 610,070,000,000,000,000 to pay for that cent. Placing these spheres in a straight row, their combined length would be 4,826,870,000,000,000,000 miles, a distance which it would take light (going at the rate of 186,330 miles per second) 820,890,000 years to travel.

The planets and stars of the entire solar and stellar universe, as seen by the great Lick telescope, if they were all in solid gold, would not nearly pay the amount. A single sphere to pay the whole amount, if placed with its centre at the sun, would have its surface extending 563,580,000 miles beyond the orbit of the planet Neptune, the farthest in our system.

It may be added that if the earth had contained a population of ten billions, each one making a million dollars a second, then to pay for that cent it would have required their combined earnings for 26,938,500,000,000,000,000,000 years.

Anyone can figure on this and see if it be correct.

Had Peter only thought to put one cent at interest, there would be no call now for Peter's pence.

With any accretion allowed, the concentration of wealth is irresistible. However small the amount of capital, if permitted to grow at any rate of increase it will ultimately absorb everything. Any finite quantity permitted any finite rate of increase, will, in finite time, gather all that is less than infinite.

The only difficulty in this accretion is to secure debtors that will not die. We inherit the property of our fathers, but fortunately we do not inherit their personal debts. This difficulty is being overcome by bonds of corporations and nations that live on, though the individuals composing them may, age after age, pass away. This makes the increase perpetual. Generations may come and go, but the concentration of wealth goes uninterruptedly on.

This is not visionary theory, but is shown in the practical results everywhere apparent.

The usurers of England, a little over two hundred years ago, secured a charter for a bank on the condition that they loan the crown or government 1,200,000 pounds sterling, about six million dollars.

This was a perpetual loan, never to be repaid, but annual interest at eight per cent. was to be paid by the government forever. This constant annual interest paid to this bank has made it such a financial power that it reaches and draws to itself of the resources of all lands. The aggregated wealth of the institution, if the accretions were continuous, would now be $25,165,824,000,000. The wealth of the United Kingdom is estimated at fifty billions, and all Europe two hundred billions, the United States seventy billions, and the whole world's wealth at five hundred billions.

Were the accretions of the bank at eight per cent. undisturbed and unconsumed, it would now take fifty worlds as rich as ours to pay that debt. It is sometimes wondered how there can be such an accumulation of wealth in one institution as to control the finances of the world.

It is often attributed to superior wisdom or some profound, occult manipulation. It is but the natural operation of the principle of interest—accretion from age to age.

The managers may be stupid dolts, only so they do not interfere with the usurious principle in its eternal pull on the resources of mankind.

The interest bearing debt of the United States, at this date, is about one thousand millions. This in one hundred years at six per cent. would amount to $340,000,000,000; five times the whole present wealth of the nation.

The smallest national bank organized, by the deposit of $25,000 of bonds yielding two per cent. interest, and permitted to re-loan the same funds to its private customers at eight per cent., could gather to itself in one hundred years, $345,225,000.

The wealth of an individual or of a family may also grow with the years as they pass. The property may be in public bonds or that of incorporations, requiring no care or effort on their part, yet it may be continually increasing. A usurer in any community in one life comes to absorb the wealth of that community, though the amount loaned at the beginning was small.

The accretions are the irresistible result of the principle of usury.

The wealth is more and more centralized as the years pass. Great trees in the forest shadow the smaller, and rob them of the sunshine and moisture until they perish. Great fish in the crowded pond feed upon the smaller. Individual manufacturers are absorbed by the great combinations called trusts. The stockholders of a railroad are absorbed by those who have large and controlling interest. But the railroad is itself absorbed by another yet greater corporation, and this again by a great combine that eliminates the influence of all but the chief control, and tends to a complete centralization of all the systems.

There is no escaping from this centralizing draft upon all resources, when the system of interest-taking is as general as now. Freedom from personal debt does not deliver us. The farmer, the most independent of men, in his own home, free from personal debt, yet must contribute to this centralizing by paying interest on bonds in every shipment of produce, and every mile of railroad travel. He pays tribute also in all the tools that he buys, in the food that he eats and the clothes that he wears.

This centralizing draft is constant, though not always equally apparent. Certain favorable conditions may hold in check, for a time, the adverse influence and cause a temporary distribution of wealth to the producers. Its force is not, however, destroyed, but only restrained for a time, and then draws with accumulated power.

Times of industrial depression and commercial disasters are occurring over and over again. Some economists attribute them to the peculiar industrial and monetary conditions of the periods in which they occur; but they have seldom agreed as to the causes of any particular panic. They are so regular in their recurrence that some economists have thought they must be produced by some constant cause; like the moon causing the tides of the ocean. Both are true. There is a general and there is also a secondary or superficial cause.

The times of greatest commercial disasters in this country were in the years 1809, 1818, 1837, 1873, 1893.

The political economists can assign as reasons some peculiar conditions prevailing in each of these periods, but the wisest have never gone deep enough to discover the general cause; this constant centralizing draft of usury.

In these periods of commercial disaster there is no destruction of property. There is only a general shake up and redistribution.

All the wealth of the country remains, but after the disaster wealth is always found to be in fewer hands. Some have become rich, many who were thought to be wealthy are ruined, and the number of the poor has been multiplied.

A patient may be afflicted with some deep-seated, chronic disease that makes him very easily affected by a change of the weather, by a change of his diet or of his bed, and these may be assigned as the causes of his frequent relapses, and they are the immediate or secondary causes, but the real cause is the deep-seated, chronic disease. Cure that disease and the changes in conditions, now so serious, would not be noticed by the healthy man.

The real and constant cause of our recurring financial disasters is this centralizing usury that directly opposes the distribution of wealth that is natural, when the producers of wealth are permitted to receive and enjoy it. Root out this evil, and then the trifling differences in our harvests, changes in our tariff laws, currency legislation, and the score of other things that now affect us, would be unfelt by the healthy body politic.

If this centralizing power is destroyed then the natural distribution would be undisturbed, and these, so-called, panics would be unknown.

CALVIN ELLIOTT

CHAPTER XXX

MAMMON DOMINATES THE NATIONS

The debt habit has been diligently cultivated and encouraged, until the nations are enslaved. Public bonds imply bondsmen, and the nations are no longer free. There is a mortgage upon the inventive genius, industry and productive energy of the world.

Usurers greatly prefer an organized government as a debtor. The individual may die, but a nation's debts bind from age to age, are bequeathed by the fathers to the children, and thus descend from generation to generation. The bonds of no corporation, however great and rich, can be so secure. They embrace special industries, while national debts are a claim upon every industry and a mortgage upon every foot of soil, and every dollar of present personal property, and of all that may be produced in the whole realm.

If we express the world's indebtedness, the national debts, in the terms of our currency, as nearly as we can reduce the currency of other nations to such an expression, we find the national debts as follows, in 1890:

Denmark	$33,004,722
Great Britain	3,848,460,000
United States	915,962,112
Germany	1,956,217,017

Austria-Hungary	$2,666,339,539
France	4,446,793,398
Russia	3,491,016,074
Italy	2,324,826,329
Spain	1,251,433,096
Netherlands	430,539,653
Belgium	360,504,099
Sweden	64,220,807
Norway	13,973,752
Portugal	490,493,599
Greece	107,306,518
Turkey	821,000,000
Switzerland	10,912,925
These debts aggregate	$22,955,386,008

Hundreds of millions have been added to these national debts in the last ten years. Nearly every nation has increased its indebtedness, possibly no nation has decreased it, and others, like China, with its recent great loan, and little Korea, with its twelve millions, must be added to the list. The debts of the nations of Europe have been increased until they now amount in the aggregate to twenty-three billions. The debts of the nations of all the world have increased one-half since 1890, and now aggregate thirty-three billions.

These great national debts are practically perpetual, and though they may be at so low a rate of interest as three per cent., they absorb the energies of the people, and, like a glacier grinding over the earth, crush all beneath them.

Public debts are incurred to relieve the present wealth of the burden of present duty. Debts place the whole burden on producers of the future. They relieve those who hold the wealth now, but are a draft upon those who make the wealth that is to be.

An individual incurring debt places a mortgage upon his productions; by a pledge of future production he relieves himself of the strain of the present.

A family incurs debt; a part of the members of the house are strong and capable of productive labor, and a part are not; the whole burden of the payment comes upon the productive members of the home. The weak and helpless and the indolent, though strong, bear no part of the burden. This family has a home, and a mortgage is placed upon it to secure the present needs. The burden of paying the interest on this mortgage, and the final payment of the principal, is wholly on the capable and industrious members of the family.

National debts are incurred to relieve the present wealth of the burden of present government calls and obligations, and to roll it upon those who shall produce wealth in the future. So the debt of a city, state, or nation is a present relief to property holders, by placing the producers under future obligations.

A street in a city is to be paved; no additional tax is levied; but bonds are issued running twenty years.

This relieves the present wealth of the burden, placing it upon those who shall produce the wealth that shall be in twenty years.

The expenses of a great war must be met. Present taxes may be slightly increased, but to meet the burden consols or public bonds are issued to be paid at a distant date. This relieves the present wealth, but binds it upon those who shall be the producers of wealth in the generations to come. Hume says, "The practice of contracting debts will almost invariably be abused by every government. It would scarcely be more imprudent to give a prodigal son a credit with every banker, than to empower statesmen to draw bills in this manner on posterity."

These public bonds are the golden opportunity of the usurers. Not only is their wealth relieved of all burden, but it affords an opportunity of profitable investment with the best possible debtor. They can pose as enterprising citizens, and urge great public improvements, and at the same time gain a most sure and profitable investment. They can pose as patriots in time of war, and urge that it be pressed with energy at whatever cost of treasure and blood. It is not their blood that is shed, nor their wealth that is wasted. It gives them the opportunity of binding their burdens on the nation for the producers of the coming generations to carry.

Usurers never wish public debts paid. They wish them issued for as long time as possible, and then reissued, or the time extended before they are due. This is done by the figment called refunding, as if it were a concession and favor to a poor debtor. It is but a device to keep the burden on the public back. It is not a financial feat and triumph for the chancellor of the exchequer to refund a public debt. He but yields himself as a tool to the usurers to continue their loans. They resist the payment when due, but when an officer is found willing to extend them before they are due all trouble is avoided and the accretions of interest are not interrupted for a day.

Those who hold the bonds of a nation direct its destinies. The nation borrowing is servant to the lender, just as an individual. The nation compromises its freedom and becomes the slave of its bond-holders. The usurers use their power for the advancement of their own material interests, and hold all other purposes of government as inferior to their own ends. This subordination of a people, to the creditors, is fatal to republican and constitutional governments; the form may be preserved for a time, but the substance of free government has departed.

The concentration of wealth carries with it the concentration of power, and is inimical to republican institutions. A proper distribution of wealth and power must be preserved or popular government is put in jeopardy.

The first bank of deposit and discount was the Bank of Venice, in the republic of Venetia. It continued its existence for six hundred years, until the government that gave it life itself perished. From its long continuous business, and its success as a bank, it has been spoken of in every work on banking as a model. It began its association with the republic in 1171, and dominated it, sapping its life, and assuming its functions, until the bank practically ruled the state, and when one fell both perished in 1797. The usurers received their hold on the state in a time of the greatest need. The republic had been impoverished by the crusades, and was in dire financial straits. Advantage was taken of this by the usurers to so bind the bank and state together that when one lived the other must, or both must die together. Stock in the bank was a loan to the state at four per cent. annual interest. The union seemed to promise great prosperity for a time, but really absorbed all the republic's vitality during the last hundred years of their life.

Venetia was at the first a pure democracy. The Doge was elected by the people and administered the government, himself being the responsible head. He, later, chose advisers, or a cabinet, to be associated in the responsible duties. After this, and about the time of the association with the bank, a representative council was elected by the people, and the government was administered by the Doge and this council. This was gradually transformed from a government of the people to an oligarchy; and as the years passed there were no steps taken toward a return, but the authority and power was more and more centralized. The ruling class was, in a hundred years, limited to those families enrolled in the "Golden Book." In another hundred years the government was in control of the "Council of Ten." Later the secret tribunal of three was the terror of the people and the instrument of their oppression. The republic was only such in name, the people were deprived of all voice in the government, and the Doge became a puppet to obey the ruling cabal.

Shakespeare went to Venice to find his typical usurer in Shylock the Jew. He found there also his typical Christian, Antonio. Antonio was a benevolent great soul, who loved his friends, supported all benevolences, and hated the usurers. Shylock hated him because he would lend without interest, and was constantly reproving him for his usurious practice.

The contest between the usurers and the people of the Venetian republic was a struggle for the life, but the usurers never relaxed their hold. They dominated until the end.

Another great triumph of the usurers was in England at the time of great need. William and Mary had been placed upon the throne by the Protestants, but were in need of money to carry on the struggle for its complete establishment. This was the usurers' opportunity. Former kings, in like straits, had confiscated the wealth of the usurious Jews, Lombards and Goldsmiths, and appropriated their property as a penalty for their unchristian practice, but William and Mary entered into a contract with them to gain their assistance, giving them special privileges to secure a permanent loan. They were to loan the crown 1,200,000 pounds sterling. This was never to be repaid, but interest at the rate of eight per cent. per annum was to be paid forever. This loan was a marvel of success. There was a great rush of usurers to place their money with the crown as a perpetual loan at that rate of increase. Their usuries, which had hitherto been counted dishonest gain, were henceforth to be honorable, and they esteemed as patriots.

Thus, the first Protestant power in the world was established in the hands of usurers, and bound to continue associated with them forever. The story, by Macauley, of the establishment of the Bank of England, is familiar to all students of English history.

This bank is a great corporation; the Board of Directors is composed of twenty-six members, who elect their own successors, and thus it is entirely independent. It makes laws for its own direction in the name of the people or defies their control. In 1797 it secured an order from the privy council ordering itself to suspend specie payment. It obeyed its own order promptly, and at the same time announced their strength and that the order would be temporary; but for one excuse and another it was continued for twenty-five years.

Sir Robert Peel, in 1844, having become convinced of the dangerous and disastrous influence, expanding and contracting its loans, secured the enactment of a law to regulate and limit its circulation. This law was distasteful to the bank, and was, upon its enactment, defied by open disobedience. It has not only dictated the laws for its own regulation, but directed both the domestic and the foreign policy of the government. It has subordinated the public weal to financial profit. This corporation of usurers manage all the finances of the kingdom, and has more influence than Crown and Parliament combined. As a great uncrowned king it dictates the diplomatic policies of the United Kingdom. Its influence has not been extended to promote Protestant Christian faith, Jews are not zealous for any Christian sect; nor for the purpose of lifting up the degraded and enlightening them; nor in the east has it exercised its power to relieve human suffering, but its diplomatic policy has been mercenary greed always.

It should be noted that the enlightened Christian people of the United Kingdom are not the English government. There has been, for two hundred years, a power behind the Throne, behind Parliament, behind the people, essentially selfish and commercial. This has controlled India for profit, while the benevolent people were anxious to christianize and uplift. It has befriended the Turk while England wept over the Turkish barbarities. It forced opium upon China while the Christian people sent missionaries. The people of England love freedom, yet the government has endeavored to crush it in the American colonies and everywhere throughout the world, when in conflict with a selfish commercial policy. The English people cry out against human slavery, yet in the struggle in the United States, when slavery was in the balance, the English government earnestly espoused the cause of those who upheld slavery. The English people rejoiced that the slave trade in Africa was abolished, yet the government enacted the hut tax, and compels now the service of the young and vigorous blacks in the mines, sending them back to their people when their strength declines.

In the establishment of the republic of the United States there was a strong resistance to any debt or subordination to usurers. The history of banks in the United States shows a struggle at the birth of the nation between the usurers, who demanded the management of the finances, and the people who resisted. This struggle continued for half a century, when the people triumphed, and for thirty years there was no hint of a purpose to overthrow what was regarded as the settled policy of the nation.

The first bank was incorporated in 1791. Its establishment was strongly resisted, but being urged by the Secretary of the Treasury, a charter was granted for twenty years. When that charter expired by limitation in 1811, there was a struggle by the usurers to secure its renewal, but they were defeated. They did not, however, abandon their effort. In 1816 they secured the charter of the second bank of the United States. This charter was also limited to twenty years, expiring in 1836. There was a tremendous struggle for its renewal, but the chief executive, backed by a strong political party, so completely defeated it that the usurers for the time yielded, and for thirty years the settled policy of the government forbade the alliance with usurers and the making of any public debt. Many of the leading statesmen of that period were very pronounced in their opposition.

"The banking system concentrates and places the power in the hands of those who control it.

"Never was an engine invented better calculated to place the destines of the many in the hands of the few, or less favorable to that equality and independence which lies at the bottom of our free institutions."—J.C. Calhoun.

"I object to the continuance of this bank because its tendencies are dangerous and pernicious to the government and the people. It tends to aggravate the inequality of fortunes; to make the rich richer, and the poor poorer; to multiply nabobs and paupers, and to deepen and widen the gulf that separates Dives from Lazarus."—Thomas H. Benton.

"I sincerely believe that banking establishments are more dangerous than standing armies. I am not among those who fear the people. They and not the rich are our dependence for continued freedom. And to preserve their independence, we must not let our rulers load us with perpetual debts."—Thomas Jefferson.

"Events have satisfied my mind, and I think the minds of the American people, that the mischief and dangers which flow from a national bank far overbalance all its advantages."—Andrew Jackson.

The usurers were compelled to remain under public condemnation during thirty years, as sentiment was strongly against them and conditions were not in their favor, but they did not relax their watchful effort nor abandon hope of ultimate success. When the nation was struggling to prevent its dissolution in 1861-5, and unusual war measures seemed necessary to meet the great emergency, the usurers saw their opportunity and came forward, as they did in Venice and England; they would loan the government the funds necessary to carry on the war, if the government would comply with their conditions and grant them the privileges demanded. They asked that their loan be perpetual, like the English loan; that they should be freed from the burdens of the government; that their loan should be free from taxation; that they should receive their interest semi-annually, and not in the common legal tender, but in coin; that they be permitted to issue their own notes as currency to be loaned to their customers; that the government discredit its own issues and endorse theirs; and that they be given a monopoly by taxing out of existence all opposition.

These were great demands, and were regarded as extortionate and oppressive. The struggle was severe, but the enemy in the field was threatening the life of the nation, while the usurers were urgent and posing as patriots, that they might accomplish their ends. True patriots, anxious to defeat the enemy in arms, regarded these usurers at home as equally the enemies of freedom. They were in a strait betwixt two foes.

Secretary McCullough said, "Hostility to the government has been as decidedly manifested in the efforts that have been made in the commercial metropolis of the nation to depreciate the currency as has been by the enemy."

The opposition to the usurers was very strong and bitter, but the conditions were in their favor and they gained a decided advantage. In the Senate the vote stood twenty-three yeas to twenty-one nays. It was carried only as a war measure. There was an effort to limit the usurers' privileges to the war and one year after its close. This was not successful, but their loan was confined to the war debt, and their time to its payment, limited to twenty years.

This action caused great distress and dark forebodings of evil to many of the thoughtful. It was setting aside the policy of the nation, which had been generally acquiesced in as wise and judicious and safe for many years. The old patriot Thadeus Stevens, in the opening of a speech in a preliminary skirmish between patriotism and usurers, said: "I approach the subject with more depression of spirits than I ever before approached any question. No personal motive or feeling influences me. I hope not, at least. I have a melancholy foreboding that we are about to consummate a cunningly devised scheme, which will carry great injury and great loss to all classes of people throughout the Union, except one." Later he said, in excuse of the action, "We had to yield, we did not yield until we found that the country must be lost or the banks gratified, and we have sought to save the country in spite of the cupidity of its wealthier classes."

The usurers have never relaxed the hold they secured by this victory, and have since been continually increasing their power. They obtained an extension or "refunding" of the war debt, and a renewal of their charters by the general laws, so their hold is indefinitely extended. Bonds are no longer limited to the covering of war expenses, but are issued freely in times of peace. The traditions of the fathers have been cast to the winds, and their fears derided and their policy changed. The usurers have been firmly in the saddle for many years, and have defeated every effort that has been made to unseat them.

The great debts of the nations have brought all mankind into subjection to the usurers. Those who hold the bonds have the destinies of the race in their hands. They pervert the ends of government; the protection of life, liberty and the highest good of all the people; they make governments their tools to gather and appropriate the earnings of the many.

They have exalted Mammon upon the throne of the world, and scoff at the God of heaven, who seeks the poor and needy, and who would in love lift up every son and daughter of the whole race.

Milton presents Mammon as one of the devils cast out of heaven with Satan, and as saying in the council of the demons,

"What place can be found for us within heaven's bound, unless heaven's Lord we overpower?... How wearisome eternity so spent in worship paid, to one we hate."

The reign of Mammon subordinates character and virtue and liberty and human life to sordid gain, yet he holds the scepter of power.

He elects legislators and senators. He elects governors or directs their arrest if they refuse to obey him. He elects presidents and dictates their policies. He places kings on their thrones and holds them there while they do his bidding. He strips a Khedive of power, and yet retains him as a collector of revenue. He steadies the Sultan's tottering throne, and compels six great Christian powers to stand by in silence while humanity is outraged. The Armenian's blood must be permitted to flow because the persecution is by a great servant, the Sultan, who pays interest on bonds, and his victims are only freemen. The murder of one hundred thousand Armenians meant nothing to Mammon. But when the Cretans were persecuted by the same Sultan, the suffering and bloodshed was soon ordered stopped by these same six powers, at Mammon's command. The Cretans were servants of the common master; the Cretan bonds were endangered. The cry of suffering humanity came up to deaf ears, but the cry of endangered bonds was heard from afar by this reigning god of wealth.

The little republics of Africa were freemen, and therefore Mammon sees them strangled with indifference. Mammon gathers the civilized nations around China and demands that she shall be enslaved by all the bonds she can safely carry or submit to vivisection and distribution.

This enslavement of the race is not by the destroying of intelligence, nor by denying the first principles of civil liberty, nor by crushing the aspirations for freedom, but by producing conditions that make the application of these principles and the exercise of freedom impossible. Though the race may increase in intelligence and theoretically have correct views of personal freedom and civil liberty, yet the conditions produced necessarily by usury utterly prevent their realization. The intelligence and aspirations of the race never were higher than at present, their subjection and subordination to material wealth was never more complete.

The scepter wherein lies Mammon's power to sway the nations is usury. When bonds bear no increase his sovereignty is gone. All motive to involve the nation in debt at once disappears, and the power to control is lost. Moses' law was divinely wise that forbade interest, that his people could not be enslaved and might remain a free people forever.

CHAPTER XXXI

EFFECT ON CHARACTER

The greatest factor in life in all ages is not material wealth, nor social position, nor genius, nor education, but character. Since man is above things, the highest purpose is not the gathering of that beneath him, but the developing of the best and noblest that is in him.

The highest possible purpose and work is the developing of virtuous manhood.

This was the thought of our fathers when they came to these shores and built their homes and established the free institutions which we now enjoy. They sacrificed material advantages that they might be free men and secure for themselves and for their children the opportunity to reach in faith and practice the ideal manhood.

No material advantage can be regarded with favor that is detrimental to the characters of men. Position, wealth, education, are worse than worthless when associated with a corrupted manhood.

"Ill fares the land, to hastening ills a prey, Where wealth accumulates, and men decay."

The test of truth is its developing of the virtues and graces. Falsehood is detected by its quickening the vices that degrade and destroy. "By their fruits shall ye know them."

Virtues are linked together so that the promoting of one gives strength to the others. All vices are also so linked that the stimulating of one quickens other vices.

Virtues and vices are opposite, so that the encouraging of a vice or fault discourages the opposing virtue. When you discourage a virtue, you encourage a vice.

The old-fashioned virtues which our fathers prized, and which they regarded essential elements of worthy manhood, were industry, and honesty, and self-reliance, and brotherly sympathy, and the devout recognition of God's divine sovereignty.

1. Usury discourages industry and encourages idleness. The laborer is stirred to diligence when he gets good wages. When his wages are meager he becomes discouraged, relaxes his efforts and may abandon his work altogether. When he knows that he is receiving less than he is earning, and that a part of his earnings are appropriated by another, he is embittered and becomes indifferent. When he receives all he earns, and the more diligent he is in his work the more he receives, he is stimulated to the utmost.

This will be especially true if it is made impossible to secure a gain without earning it. The benefit of full wages may be largely lost by the knowledge of persons who, without productive effort, are appropriating the earnings of others. The influence of their easy, indolent lives may destroy or counteract the beneficent influence of good wages. The laborer may be led to despise his well-paid tasks and yearn for their ease, and thus become indolent.

One is encouraged to idleness when he discovers that he can secure his bread by the sweat of another's face. He is likely to relax his efforts if he does not forsake all personal productive occupations. He may give great care and the closest attention to the management of his wealth, loaning to others and collecting the increase, but not to productive industry.

There are activities that look like virtues, but they are perverted efforts. The slave-driver may work as hard as the slave in his efforts to appropriate the earnings of others. The thief may work in the night and endure more hardness to secure the property of another than would be necessary to honestly earn it. The usurer may give his thought, night and day, to the placing of his wealth the most securely and at the best rates of interest, and at the same time abandon all effort in the direct management of useful productive enterprises.

The complete result of usury upon the habit of industry can be realized in those who have grown up under its influence; those who have an income secure from invested funds. When there is no need, present nor prospective, there is no motive to active industry, and the love of ease and pleasure grows and drives out all heart for productive effort.

The industrious habit coupled with economy is called thrift. It is not parsimony or unwillingness to give, but a disposition to save. Our Lord, who was the prince of givers and inculcated unlimited giving among his followers, gave a lesson in thrift when he said after his miracle, "Gather up the fragments, that nothing be lost."

Enforced industry and economy is not thrift. When by low wages or grinding conditions the necessities of life are with difficulty secured, the very opposite disposition may be cultivated. When the external restraints are removed, the wildest extravagance may be indulged in. This is sometimes given as an excuse for low, grinding wages; that "the workmen and their wives have no idea of saving;" that higher wages would be wasted in foolish extravagance.

No one in normal conditions will be wasteful of that which has cost him hard labor. His care for it will naturally be in proportion to the effort that was necessary to secure it. Those who waste the wealth of the world are not those who by the sweat of their faces have produced it. The habit of thrift comes from the knowledge of the value of a thing, learned by earning it. Only that which comes without effort will be spent without thought. Those who have livings secured from the increase or interest of "productive" capital, having no need of industry, are wholly occupied with the spending; but in spending only, the value of the thing spent is not appreciated, the habit of extravagance grows and they become the idlers and the spendthrifts of the world.

2. It prevents open and frank honesty. When the thought is turned to an endeavor to secure a dollar that is not earned, there is secretiveness of purpose and inward guile. No person doing business on borrowed capital advertises the number and amount of his loans nor does he welcome inquiry by others. In a column of advertisements by money lenders in a newspaper lying on this table every one promises "privacy" or "no publicity." No one can be so open and frank as the one who earns every dollar that he receives or seeks.

The possibility of speculation is ruinous. The first step in the wreck of integrity in a young man's character is when he becomes absorbed in some scheme by which he can secure gain without honestly earning it. Lotteries are outlaws not only because they defraud but they undermine integrity and honest industry.

When property earns property, and the gain is secured with no struggle on his part, the temptation is presented and the disintegration of his character has begun. When there is no gain except by production, the whole thought and energy of the man is directed to that end, and his desire to secure that earned by another is restrained. The frank, open disposition is preserved. Honest productive toil drives out the spirit of speculation. Under usury, both lender and borrower are in the attitude of expectants of unearned gain.

3. It discourages the spirit of self-reliance.

Usury causes a broad separation between a man of property and the man of mere muscle or brain. It makes such large combinations of capital possible in immense shops and department stores and other enterprises, that the individual workman is belittled. Under the principle of usury, property can produce as well as brain or muscle. One having property can control both.

His property places him in a position as a superior. He comes to forget the relations he bears to men as equals, and requires that those who have only their natural gifts shall be cringing supplicants before him or be denied his favor. The borrower or the laborer who asserts his rights is endangered by the man controlling property, who has him in his power.

That independent, self-reliant spirit, that looks every man in the face as an equal yet lingers in the country among the hills and mountains, but is fast disappearing from the city. There has come to the laborer in the town or city a feeling of dependence upon others and a desire to secure their favor. They almost feel that they must apologize for being laborers, and beg for an opportunity to earn a living in some one's employ. One of the saddest facts, and most threatening of disaster in these present commercial conditions, is the common desire to be employed, to get a job, dependent on the whim of another, instead of a determination to direct one's own labor and be the manager of one's own business. The sound educational development is wanting in the daily occupation of the hired laborer, and there is a loss of manhood that has no compensation.

The independent spirit slips away so gradually that its going is scarcely noticed, but when once gone the degradation is complete.

A family of free Hebrews went down into Egypt, and for a long time was in favor with the rulers, but they gradually lost their independence and became more and more servile and cringing until the Egyptian masters dared to go into their homes and pick up their boy babies and take them out and drown them as if they were worthless puppies.

The hopelessness of the Ottoman Empire today is more in the cringing subordination and broken spirit of the people than in the oppression of the Sultan. His government might be overthrown in a day, but it would take ages to lift up that empire of prostrate slaves and to cultivate in them the self-assertion and self-reliance necessary to a free people.

Every man who loves his country and his race must view with alarm this growing feeling of subordination and cringing disposition. It is the very reverse of that democratic spirit or consciousness of equality that must prevail to secure the permanency of our republican institutions.

4. It destroys fraternal sympathy. Two classes are found in every modern community. The one is the laborers with muscle or brain, the other class, those whose property produces for them. Between these classes there is a great wall fixed. It cannot be expected that they will mingle harmoniously and be in sympathy in civil and social relations. Producing and non-producing classes can never be congenially associated.

The question is frequently discussed in church circles, "How can the laboring man be attracted to the churches?" The discussion often presumes that the non-laboring man does find the church congenial. If he does, all efforts to win the other class will be in vain. The church itself needs to correct its teachings and reform its spirit.

The moral law commands "Six days shalt thou work," and there is no release because a man has property. So long as a man has brain or brawn he is bound by that law. If he is not, he is not a moral man, and has no rightful place in the church of God. Honest, upright, industrious Christian men, engaged in all lines of production for human needs, may be congenial and co-operate most harmoniously, but they never can be made comfortable in association with those who are unproductive and idle, yet living in luxury.

5. Usury promotes that "Covetousness which is idolatry."

"As heathens place their confidence in idols, so doth the avaricious man place his confidence in silver and gold. The covetous person, though he doth not indeed believe his riches or his money to be God, yet by so loving and trusting in them, as God alone ought to be loved and trusted in, he is as truly guilty of idolatry as if he so believed."

Idolatry is the act of ascribing to things or persons properties that are peculiar to God. The principal objects of worship are those things which bring to men the greatest good.

The sun has been the most general object of idolatrous worship in all the ages. It is the most conspicuous object, and is the source of light and heat, and rules the seasons. Its worship was so general that the Hebrew people, when they lapsed from the worship of God, turned to the worship of the sun or Baal. No natural object is more worthy of worship. Job declaring his integrity and freedom from idolatry, said that he had not kissed his hand in salute of the sun in his rising.

The river Nile was an object of idolatrous worship for ages. Its source was a mystery, and its annual rise in its rainless valley was so beneficent, that it was given the worship which belonged to the Divine alone. All the hope of the harvest depended on its annual overflow. It moistened and fertilized and prepared the ground, and then receded until the harvest was grown and gathered. Moses showed the Egyptians the impotence of their idols by making this chief idol, and the things that came out of it, a curse. The cow was worshiped because it was the most useful and necessary of their animals. A real or supposed power to give or withhold favors has been from the beginning the source and spring of idolatry.

Riches, property, as the means of supplying our needs, is an object more coveted than any other. The principle of usury greatly aggravates this tendency. The principle of usury makes it imperishable; it can be perpetuated, unimpaired from year to year and from age to age; it is a constant source of benefit; it is productive of all that is necessary to supply human needs.

It supplies, too, without effort on the part of the recipient. The sun, with his light and heat, makes the labor of the farmer successful. The rising Nile moistening and fertilizing the land, prepares the way for the sower. The cow draws the plow and the harrow, and threshes the grain, but usury makes property bring all needed material good without effort on the part of the owner. It brings him the matured fruits of the farm, though he neither plows or sows nor reaps. No labor on his part is needed. His property clothes and feeds him, and yet does not grow less, but is endowed with perpetual youth, ever giving yet never exhausted or diminished. He may die, but his idol knows no decay, and may continue to bless his children through the generations. This quality of riches makes them a greater source of blessing than the sun or any other object of idolatrous worship. This leads to unlimited self-denial and sacrifice to gain and retain property. The devotees subordinate their own ease and physical comfort, their own intellectual development, to secure it, they will themselves shrivel in body and soul; like other idolaters they will even yield the highest interests of their children, when this idol demands their sacrifice.

6. It destroys spirituality. Property is matter and not spirit. With the thought and heart and effort directed to a material thing, the spirit is neglected. The heathen Greek artist directed his whole attention to the material part of man. The symmetry of the human physical form was his study. The perfect man was the most symmetrically developed specimen of physical form. His thought of man was matter. The Christian directs his thought to the spirit, his mind and heart, his noble purposes, and all the qualities of true manhood. The material part is subordinated to the spiritual.

The tendency now is to appreciate a man for what he has rather than for what he is, to ignore both symmetry of form and the graces of the noble character, and to worship what he holds in his hands. The truly spiritual loves true manhood and is indifferent to the possessions.

If a noble soul is found in a Lazarus, the true child of Abraham will take him to his bosom. A perverted manhood will receive no favor though clothed and surrounded with all material splendor.

It destroys spirituality, too, because it holds the mind to a material thing as the source of all good. The spiritual man rises to the true source of our blessings, the author of all temporal good, from whose hand every living thing is fed.

This, as all idolatry, leads to a breaking away from the restraints of the moral law. The devotion to the material leads, logically and practically, to a neglect of the restraints of the spiritual, and a preponderance of subserviency to the material. Practices that will promote the material are indulged though the moral law may be broken. The material is not held subject to the needs of the higher nature, nor subject to the promotion of the kingdom of God, but man's noblest gifts and the worship of God are all made, if possible, to minister to the material interests.

To break this idol's power, the true nature of property must be shown. It is not immortal, but perishable. It can not preserve itself, but must be carefully preserved by man's own effort. It can not protect him, but he must protect it. It is but a thing which man has himself made. It must be shown absurd, as Isaiah ridiculed it, "They worship the work of their own hands, that which their own fingers have made."

Other forms of gross external idolatry are exposed by the advancing light of these progressive years, but this musty old form has taken new life and now receives the service of the race. The whole world is running pell-mell after this idol. It stands in the market places, it is not a stranger in the courts of justice, and is in high favor in legislative halls. Solon is relegated and Croesus is elected.

It is given a high place in the temple of God. Pious Lazarus is neglected but Dives is promoted.

"What agreement hath the temple of God with idols?"

Until this idol is cast out the church will and must languish. Spiritual life will be low and fervor impossible.

CHAPTER XXXII

AX AT ROOT OF THE TREE

I t is easier to cut down an evil tree than to climb up and lop
off it branches; besides the branches will grow again if the
stock is left undisturbed. It is easier to destroy the mother
of vipers than it is to chase after, catch and kill her poisonous
progeny. The reptiles will not become extinct while the mother
is left to breed without restraint. There are a large number of
industrial and financial evils that derive their strength from
usury, which have received the close attention of benevolent
reformers, but they have not exposed the cause, nor have they
suggested a sufficient remedy. That the evils exist is apparent to
them all, but they seem too high to reach or too swift to be
caught.

It is only possible to hint at the prevailing evils in one chapter.
It would require a volume to discuss them in detail and to apply
the remedy.

1. There is a tendency to divergence in the material and
financial conditions of men. Some are growing richer, while
others are growing poorer.

The prayer of Agur, "Give me neither poverty nor riches," is
the prayer we should offer and the prayer we should try
ourselves to answer. We are to seek freedom from poverty on
the one hand and from ensnaring riches on the other. This is
the condition we should try to secure in the community and in
the commonwealth. We should discourage excess of riches and

we should endeavor to relieve all of distressing poverty. We should hedge about accumulation with such conditions as to make it very difficult to gain great wealth, and at the same time we should so ease the conditions of accumulation that only gross indolence or great misfortune could cause dependent poverty.

The so called middle class are those who neither have great riches nor yet are they in fear of want. The great mass of our people belonged to this class until very recent times. Now we find the excessively rich have multiplied and a vast number of our industrious, honest and virtuous population are struggling for life's necessities. The middle class is less numerous while both those in opulence and those in poverty have been increasing.

We should level up and level down to the medium which is best for the development of the highest manhood and best also for the strength and perpetuity of our republican institutions.

The rich should be limited in their accretions while the poor are lifted out of their poverty; but how can this be accomplished without interfering with individual liberty and our personal rights? The problem is not easily solved. While usury remains, which is an ever active centralizing force adding wealth to wealth, no remedy can be found. Do away with usury, and the evil is overcome.

(*a*) When it is recognized that vital energy alone produces all wealth, no great fortune can be gathered in the life time of one man. The earnings of any life, however long, or the earnings of a succession of industrious, energetic ancestors, could not amass a fortune to interfere with the rights and activities of others.

One may inherit a large fortune from wealthy kindred; he may discover a fortune; he may draw a grand prize in a lottery; he may as a Turk seize the properties of others and then bribe the courts to confirm his claims; or a people may be "held up" by law and one, selfish and conscienceless as a ghoul, may jump at the opportunity and appropriate their earnings and their property and yet the robber keep out of the penitentiary; but no one, however great his skill or brilliant his genius, can earn one million dollars, nor the tenth of it, in his natural life. To gain one million dollars one must earn twenty thousand dollars each year for fifty years and save it all. He must spend nothing for pleasure nor benevolence. He must spend nothing for food nor for clothes.

(*b*) Wealth decays unless cared for and preserved. As wealth increases, the task of protecting and preserving it increases. There comes a time when production must cease, and all energy will be required to preserve that already gained. When others preserve and pay a price for the privilege, as in usury, the vital energy can continue production, indefinitely.

(*c*) Abolish usury and the instant one ceases to produce he begins to consume that which he has earned. He can not live upon the increase of his earnings, but he must begin at once to diminish the supply. Exacting usury he may consume only the increase and preserve the principal untouched. He may not consume all the increase and add the remainder to his capital and thus grow richer in decrepit age. Many of those who have not inherited wealth, have not been wealthy until advanced age. It came to them by the accretions of interest after the productive period of life was past.

(*d*) It is not possible to secure perfect equality of conditions. If all wealth was equally distributed today differences would begin to appear tomorrow. This has seemed to some disheartening and they abandon all hope of correcting the evil. They should look deeper and promote the natural and God-ordained remedy.

The natural force for the preservation of the level of the ocean is gravity. But the surface is seldom smooth. The winds lash it into fury and pile high its waves, but gravity pulling upon every drop of water tends to draw it back to its place and smooth down the surface again. The wind cannot build permanently a mountain of water in the ocean.

The consumption and decay of wealth tends unendingly to equalize the conditions of men. In the wild rush of the struggle for supremacy and gain, like a whirlwind in the affairs of men, with their diverse gifts and tastes and plans, there will be inequalities appearing, but consumption and inevitable decay are ever present leveling powers. Usury suspends this beneficent law and aggravates the evil, making the differences in condition permanent and increasing them.

Do away with usury and there is a natural limitation to riches. The rich will find that he can not grow constantly richer; not because he is by statute deprived of any personal rights, but he is hindered by the natural law embedded in things by the Creator.

Do away with usury and the problem of poverty is solved. If we credit vital energy with the increase of wealth and give the laborer all he earns, he has a fair and equal chance, and equity requires no more. It is justice and opportunity, a fair chance, that the poor need, not pity and gifts of charity.

2. Great combines of capital in business and especially in industrial trusts are receiving the closest attention of the thoughtful. Some regard them as the necessary result of successful and enlarging business. Many others regard them as hostile to the public good and are anxiously seeking a means of restraining their great and increasing power.

These were at the first associations of manufacturers who co-operated to maintain prices. In the competitive system there is a constant pressure on the part of the consumer for lower prices. The manufacturer who is conscientious and a model employer, seeking to maintain prices sufficiently high to afford him a profit and living wages for his employes, must ever be resisting this pressure. They united for this purpose and were benevolent and just in their design. But the manufacturers were paying tribute on borrowed capital. They must meet the demands of interest on their debts and also the wages of their workmen. Between these two they struggled to secure for themselves comfortable wages. The capitalists, seeing the advantage of this co-operation and the resultant profits, undertook and accomplished the combination of their capital to secure for themselves the profits at first sought for the operators and their employes.

These great combines are the natural result of successful business with the practice of usury. They threaten evil.

The purpose and plan of the present trust is to increase the increase of the capital; to make the capital more productive; to bring larger returns for the wealth invested.

(*a*) They are not organized for the benefit of the laborer. The object is to decrease the cost by producing with less labor. The less the labor, other things being equal, the greater the returns for the capital invested.

(*b*) They are not organized for the benefit of the consumer. When they do favor the consumer it is only incidental and generally temporary to meet competition. They make no pretence of being benevolent in their purposes. They are organized for the purpose of business gain.

(*c*) These capitalists combine their interests because they can thereby secure a greater return from their investments than they can by operating separately. They combine that they may mutually increase the rate of interest or dividends on their capital. This is the motive that draws them into coöperation.

The learned and benevolent statesmen, teachers of economy and reformers, have not suggested an adequate remedy. The remedy is not far to find. Do away with usury and they will fall apart like balls of sand; the cohesive power will be gone; the centralization will cease and the wealth will speedily return to the various individuals from whom it was gathered. This remedy may seem heroic, but it is a specific and is the simplest of all possible methods.

3. How to secure a just distribution of the great advantages from improved machinery, new inventions and new discoveries, is a problem that is engaging the best thought of many of the wise and good. That the present distribution is inequitable and unfair; that it gives the capitalist an undue advantage over the laborer; that it aggravates the difference in conditions, seems generally admitted.

An improved machine, owned by a capitalist, enables one man to do the work that formerly required ten. One man is employed and the nine are in competition for his place and there is no advance over the wages before the machine was introduced. The owner of the machine secures the gain. His wealth is greatly increased while the laborer plods on with his old wages. With the new machine the one man produces what ten men did before, but the product of the nine are credited to the machine and becomes the capitalist's gain.

(*a*) The falsehood on which this claim rests must be seen and rejected before the evil can be overcome; that the machine is productive. It is but a tool in the hands of the one man, who now with it produces as much as ten men did without it. If one does the work of ten he earns the reward of ten. Because by this machine he multiplies his strength, and adds to his efficiency, he can not justly be deprived of his full reward.

(*b*) "But the machine is owned by another." His not owning the machine does not change its nature and make it a productive force. Whether it belongs to him or to another, it is his intelligent vital energy that produces all that is produced. The machine is but his tool with which he works.

(*c*) "But the machine must be paid for." Certainly, the inventors and skilled mechanics, who produced this wonderful tool, should be fully compensated, but once paid they have no claim upon it or on what another may produce with it. No honest workman objects to paying a good price for good tools. It is not the purchase of tools by one set of workmen of another that causes the unequal conditions.

(*d*) It is the usurer or interest taker that perverts the conditions.

He lays hold of those great inventions and discoveries, like railroads and telegraphs and telephones, and demands a perpetual compensation. He asks that the laborer shall be forever buying his tool, yet it shall be never bought, that the public shall be forever paying for privileges and the obligation remain forever unmet. This is but one of the forms of usury, by which wealth is heaped from the earnings of the many.

4. The difficulties between employers and their laborers do not cease. The continued strikes and lock-outs show how general and deep the trouble is. Laborers organize into unions to protect themselves from discharge and to promote their interests. They ask for better wages and shorter hours. They urge their petition with forceful arguments; they make demands with an implied threat; they stop work or "strike." Then follows a test of strength and endurance in which both parties greatly suffer and both are embittered and neither is satisfied.

The correction of this common evil has received close study from those who have the welfare of all classes at heart and wish to be benefactors of the race. The remedies have not been thorough but superficial, and the benefits temporary. The branches have been cut off but they grow again.

(*a*) The complaint of too small wages implies that more is earned than is received; but there is no standard recognized by which what a man does earn can be measured. The capitalist claims the output as the earnings of his capital and his claim is allowed by the workmen. The workmen may claim that wages are too small for a comfortable living. This is not a plea of free workmen, but of slaves begging to be better fed.

(*b*) They may complain of too many hours of labor; but the number of hours of labor is arbitrarily fixed. There is no valid constant reason why one should wish to work less. In the management of one's own work, and the collection of his own earnings, there are times when long hours, of the strain of labor, are necessary, and there are other times when ease can be taken. With no standard of earnings or time, it is impossible to arrive at a just and satisfactory settlement.

The reasons given sound to the employers like the pleadings of servants for richer food and more play.

(*c*) The laborer should find a solid basal reason for his demands. That will be found only in the utter rejection of the theory and practice of usury.

The selfishness of human nature will remain; conflicts between men in all conditions and all businesses will remain; feuds and rivalries will remain; but when employer and employe are enabled to see that capital is dead, and decaying, and that all the earnings above its preservation belong to the laborers, there will be a recognized and true basis upon which the rightful claims of each can be adjusted.

(*d*) In a co-operative shop, where the workmen are the owners, each receives his share of the gains. With usury done away it is possible for workmen, who are poor, to ultimately become the owners, by the accumulation of earnings, but under the pull of the usurers, continually appropriating the earnings, they are doomed to hopeless poverty.

5. There is a widespread determination to overcome the evil of war. Non-combatants are numerous and peace societies are organized in all lands. Their literature is widely distributed and their petitions, for the preservation of peace, are poured upon every "power" that is thought to have an occasion, or a disposition, to engage in warfare. The waste of treasure and blood, the cruelties and suffering that are a military necessity, are pleaded in favor of peace. The shame of intelligent rational men settling differences with brute force is presented.

The unchristian spirit, that in this age of light and saving grace should be so wanting in brotherly love as to wish to destroy those who harm us, is deprecated.

When differences do arise between nations, they urge a just settlement or mutual concessions. Or if one is found to be unreasonable, unjust and oppressive, it is better and more christian-like, they claim, to endure hardness, submitting under protest, than by force, which the Master forbade, attempt to establish righteousness.

Rulers of the greatest nations on the earth have become conscious of the cruel burdens upon their people, in the support of their great armaments. On the invitation of the Czar of Russia, peace commissioners from many nations recently met in The Hague, to devise means by which the burdens of armaments might be diminished and actual warfare avoided. This peace council advised that differences be submitted to arbitration, but while it was yet speaking two Christian powers, began open war, without having so "decent a regard to the opinions of mankind" as to make known to the world the cause of their conflict. Wars continue, and among the most highly civilized and enlightened and christianized, in the face of the arguments and advice and pleadings of non-combatants and peace societies and peace commissions.

Mammon, a sordid greed of gain, is now on the world's throne and directs the movements of the nations in peace or war.

His purposes may be often accomplished in peace by purchases of territory for which interest bearing bonds are issued. The irritation or hurts between peoples may be mollified and healed by indemnities, which also serve his purpose because they necessitate the incurring of a bonded debt, interest bearing. But the history of the world for centuries proves that a condition of war is Mammon's opportunity to foist a debt upon a free people and to increase the burden of those whose bonds he already holds.

His ears are deaf to advice and reason, when material and commercial advantages are to be secured. He cares not for human suffering and shed blood, if riches can be increased. When concessions can be secured, and mortgages placed, and a people exploited with profit, the cry of suffering, the pleading for pity and the call for justice are all in vain.

To stop these modern wars they must be made unprofitable to Mammon. When they are made to deplete his treasury and to waste his wealth, instead of increasing it, he will call a halt in strife, and the gentle spirit of peace will be permitted to hover over the nations.

Away with national debts and interest bearing bonds, which are the delight of the usurers. Make present wealth bear the burden of present duty. Try the patriotism of the usurers by making war a real sacrifice of their wealth, while the blood of others is being poured upon the field. Do not permit war to be an advantage to the rich to increase his riches. A patriot's life is given and it goes out forever, let wealth be no more sacred than life; let it not be borrowed but consumed. Let the rich grow poorer as the war goes on, let there be a facing of utter poverty, as the patriot faces death on the field.

While Mammon is permitted this usury, his chief tool, he will use it for the oppression of the world. He will direct the movements among the nations to further his ends, although it may require a conflict between the most christianized and enlightened of the earth. The nations will be directed in peace or put in motion in war to make wealth increase.

Give wealth its true place as a perishable thing, instead of a productive life, and wars will cease in all the earth. The holders of the wealth of the world will never urge nor encourage war, when the property destroyed is their own and not to be replaced. When wars are no longer the usurer's opportunity, but the consumption of his wealth, Mammon himself will beg that swords may be beaten into plow-shares and spears into pruning-hooks.

CHAPTER XXXIII

PER CONTRA; CHRISTIAN APOLOGISTS

Every argument favoring the continuance of the practice of usury can be met from the propositions established in the preceding chapters. Indeed, there are no true arguments to be presented in its favor. Truth is consistent with truth. We are not placed in a dilemma and compelled to decide which are the strongest of the arguments arrayed against each other. We are not deciding which is the greater of two blessings nor which the less of two evils, but this is a question of evil or good, of sin or righteousness. If usury is wrong then every argument brought forward to support it is a falsehood, though it may be covered with a very beautiful and attractive and plausible form in its presentation.

1. The old Wilson Catechism published in Dundee in 1737 is perhaps the most familiar defense.

"Q. Is the gaining of money by usury unlawful?

"A. Yes, Prov. 28:8. Psalm 15:5.

"Q. What is usury?

"A. The taking unlawful profit for money that is lent out.

"Q. Is it lawful to take any interest or gain for money lent?

"A. Yes, when it is taken according to the laws of the land, and from these who make gain by it, by trading or purchasing of lands; seeing it is equally just for the owner of money to ask a share of the profit which others make by it, as for the owner of the land to demand farm from the tenant of it, money being improvable by art and labor as well as land.

"Q. What is the unlawful profit for money, which may be called usury?

"A. The taking profit for money from the poor who borrow for mere necessity, or taking needful things from them in pawn for it; or the taking more profit for any than law allows, as these who take ten, fifteen, or twenty in the hundred. Exod. 22:25, 26. Deut. 24:12, 17. Ezek. 18:7, 8.

"Q. But were not the people of Israel discharged to take any usury or profit for lent money from their brethren? Deut. 23:19.

"A. This law seems to have been peculiar to the Jewish state, and that in regard of their estates being so divided, settled, and secured to their families by the year jubilee, and their not being employed in trading or making purchases like other nations, so that they had no occasion to borrow money but for the present subsistence of their families. But for strangers, who had another way of living, the Israelites were allowed to lend upon usury, and to share with them in their profits, Deut. 23:20, which shows that the taking of interest is not oppressive in itself; for they are frequently prohibited to oppress a stranger, and yet allowed to take usury from him. Exod. 22:21, and 23:9."

The reader will notice that the definition of usury is defective. The reader will also notice that there are no Scripture references given to prove that any interest can be taken. This is singular, since throughout the Catechism Scripture references are profuse in confirmation of the answers. If a single passage had been found that could be twisted into an approval the reference would have been given. He rests the permission to take usury wholly on human reason, though in direct opposition to the Scripture references he had first given to prove that the gaining of wealth by usury was unlawful. He does not claim to get this answer from the Bible. He rests this answer on the law of the land and the purposes of the borrower, and says it is not worse than taking a rental for land anyway.

The questions with regard to the customs of the people of Israel are completely met in the Second and Third Chapters of this book.

Fisher, also, we find from his catechism published in 1753, thought it necessary to make some excuse for the custom in his time. High interest he finds condemned, but moderate interest he tries to defend.

"Q. 32. What is it to take usury, according to the proper signification of the word?

"A. It is to take gain, profit, or interest, for the loan of money.

"Q. 33. What kind of usury or interest is lawful?

"A. That which is moderate, easy, and no way oppressive. Deut. 23:20, compared with Ex. 22:21.

"Q. 34. How do you prove that moderate usury is lawful?

"A. From the very light of nature, which teaches, that since the borrower proposes to gain by the loan, the lender should have a reasonable share of his profit, as a recompense for the use of his money, which he might otherwise have disposed of to his own advantage. 1 Cor. 8:13.

"Q. 35. What is the usury condemned in scripture and by what reason?

"A. It is the exacting of more interest or gain for the loan of money, than is settled by universal consent, and the laws of the land. Prov. 28:8. 'He that by usury, and unjust gain, increaseth his substance, shall gather it for him that will pity the poor.'

"Q. 36. How do you prove from scripture, that moderate usury, or common interest, is not oppression in itself?

"A. From the express command laid upon the Israelites not to oppress a stranger, Ex. 23:9; and yet their being allowed to take usury from him, Deut. 23:20; which they would not have been permitted to do, if there had been an intrinsic evil in the thing itself.

"Q. 37. Is it warrantable to take interest from the poor?

"A. By no means; for, if such as are honest, and in needy circumstances, borrow a small sum towards a livelihood, and repay it in due time, it is all that can be expected of them; and therefore the demanding of any profit or interest, or even taking any of their necessaries of life in pledge, for the sum, seems to be plainly contrary to the law of charity. Ex. 22:25-28. Ps. 15:5.

"Q. 38. Were not the Israelites forbidden to take usury from their brethren, whether poor or rich? Deut. 23:19: 'Thou shalt not lend upon usury to thy brother.'

"A. This text is to be restricted to their poor brethren, as it is explained, Ex. 22:25, and Lev. 25:35, 36; or, if it respects the Israelites indifferently, then it is one of the judicial laws peculiar to that people, and of no binding force now."

In the answer to the 34th question he appeals to the light of nature. That light, as he interprets it, may be applied as follows. We follow his language closely and his argument perfectly.

From the very light of nature which teaches, that since the borrower of the hoe purposes to dig his own garden with it, the lender should have a reasonable amount of his garden dug, as a recompense for the use of the hoe, which he might otherwise have used himself to dig his own garden.

Fisher confirms his conclusion with a Scripture reference but it is so irrelevant that it would seem Wilson was wiser in omitting Scripture reference altogether. 1 Cor. 8:13, "Wherefore, if meat make my brother to offend, I will eat no meat while the world standeth, lest I make my brother to offend."

The only explanation the writer ever saw or heard of, that was seriously made was this: "If using my brother's money without interest offends him, then I will never while the world standeth accept his money without interest lest I make my brother to offend." If this is the intended application then it may be further applied. If using a brother's money at six per cent. offends him then I will surely give him ten per cent. lest I cause my brother offence. Could there be a more absurd application of a Scripture passage?

The later theologians have seldom mentioned usury and none have discussed it at any length, and no divine to our knowledge has undertaken a defence. The "Systematic Theology" of Dr. Charles Hodge is perhaps the most elaborate and exhaustive. He does not more than refer to usury; he does not even mention it by name. But in his discussion of the violation of the eighth commandment, he ridicules the idea that "a thing is worth what it is worth to the man who demands it." He says: "If this be so, then if a man perishing from thirst is willing to give his whole estate for a glass of water it is right to exact that price; or if a man in danger of drowning should offer a thousand dollars for a rope, we might refuse to throw it to him for a less reward. Such conduct every man feels is worthy of execration."

He closes the discussion of the eighth commandment with this significant and emphatic sentence: "Many who have stood well in society and even in the church will be astonished at the last day to find the word 'Thieves' written after their names in the great book of judgment."

2. "To prohibit usury is revolutionary."

Revolutions are not necessarily evil. They have been justified in all the ages to overthrow tyranny and oppression and to secure freedom and establish justice. Oppressors and evil-doers in power have ever been anxious to maintain the "statu quo": that is, to be let alone. The "Man of Galilee" is the prince of revolutionists. He has overthrown and turned down the civilizations of the world and has brought in his own, called by his name, Christian civilization. His followers were revolutionists. The idolatrous craftsmen of Ephesus, not wishing to be disturbed in their profitable business, in order to defeat the work of Paul and his associates, raised the cry of revolution. "These that have turned the world upside down have come hither also."

The things that are wrong side up must be revolved. When material things are found superior to true manhood and womanhood, they must be reversed. When the works of men's hands are given a place above the hands that formed them, when the results of labor are given a place above the vital energy of the laborer, there is call for revolution.

But this revolution should be the most peaceful the world ever saw. This need not require the destruction of any property nor the shedding of one drop of blood. It need interfere with no man's rights nor enforce upon any man a burden he should not be willing to bear. A man is not interfering with the rights of another when he is paying his debts, and a man should not feel that there is placed upon him a burden he is unwilling to carry, when his own property is returned to him. Yet that is the ultimate, the extreme goal, to be reached by the abolition of usury; every man free from debt and every man caring for his own property.

3. "If usury is not permitted, the great modern enterprises are impossible."

A great modern enterprise that is not for the general good has no right to be. Splendid enterprises are often made possible by the sacrifice of the welfare of the many for the interests of the few. The splendid plantations of the southern states flourished in time of slavery, when the labor of many was subordinate to the welfare of one. They are not now possible; yet the present and future general good is better secured by the sacrifice of the splendid past. A splendid military campaign is only possible by the complete subordination of the many to the will and order of the commanding head. One hundred thousand in an army is now receiving the attention of the world. One hundred thousand in happy homes are commonplace. The pyramids are splendid monuments, but they were not a blessing to the slaves, who built them.

Splendid enterprises in which the few command the many may be an unmitigated curse.

"Ye friends to truth, ye statesmen who survey The rich man's joys increase, the poor's decay; 'Tis yours to judge, how wide the limits stand, Between a splendid and a happy land."

No enterprise, however brilliant, can be in the model state, that blesses the few by the losses of the many.

Great and benign enterprises are possible without usury. There is no greater enterprise than the postal system in this land and extending to all the nations in the postal union. You owe it nothing; like poor Richard, "you pay as you go." It owes nothing, pays no interest and renders a great service for the small amount you pay. It is a standing illustration of the success of a strictly cash business.

The great benevolent missionary enterprises, that send their messengers to all lands, over the whole earth, receive and disburse the gifts of the benevolent. Their work is not interrupted, but continues from age to age.

The commerce of the world can be carried on just as effectively without usury. A mortgage does not make a farm more productive nor does a bonded debt make a railroad or a navigation company more efficient. The railroads and express and telegraph and telephone and other enterprises are greatly hindered in the service of the public by the tribute they are returning to the usurers. Had this farmer not this mortgage he could improve his farm and bring from his land better results. Were it not for the unceasing drain upon the income of great enterprises to meet the interest on bonds, the properties could be improved and the public better served at greatly reduced rates. Indeed the most successful enterprises are now operated by the owners.

4. "It will be hard to borrow, if you will not pay interest."

It would be a happy condition if no one should want to borrow except in urgent need from an accidental strait; if that old independent, self-reliant spirit that refused to be indebted to any man could be universal, that preferred frank and honest poverty in a cabin, to a sham affluence in a mortgaged palace.

It should be hard to borrow, but easy to pay. Usury makes it easy to borrow, but hard to repay. Usurers even make it attractive and entice the victim into the trap of debt and then it is all but impossible to find a way out. An honest, industrious man of good habits must be ever on the alert or he will be entangled, sooner or later, with debts.

It will not be harder for an honest man, who is in need, to borrow. He will not be able to borrow more than his need requires. The debt will not increase during the period of disability, and it will be easier to repay without increase. The usurer requires more than honesty for the security of his loan. The loan to him is precious seed, that must be planted where it will grow. To merely have the loan returned without increase does not meet his claim. To remit the increase, to make it easier for the poor debtor to pay, he would regard as a positive loss to himself and a gift to his victim. The usurer prefers rich debtors, who have abundant property to secure the loan and its increase.

There is a despised class of pawn usurers who prey upon the poor. They are regarded as robbers of the poor in their distresses, but their business would be impossible, were it not that all avenues of relief are closed by usury; "interest must be paid anywhere; why not borrow of them though the rates are high?" The moral quality of the act is the same; the difference is wholly in the degree of turpitude.

CHAPTER XXXIV

PER CONTRA; LAND RENTALS

" If no interest should be charged on money, then no rents should be collected."

The early Christian apologists for usury, who felt it imperative to explain why it was permitted and practiced among Christians, found few arguments. They all agreed that the letter and spirit of the Scriptures forbade lending to the poor, upon interest. They also found it impossible to show from reason the right of money to an increase, but as money can readily be changed into other forms of property, as lands, they reversed the arguments; beginning with the assumed premise that it is right to charge rental for lands, and as money may represent lands, it is therefore right, they say, to charge interest on money.

"It seems as lawful for a man to receive interest for money, which another takes pains with, improves, but runs the hazard in trade, as it is to receive rent for our land, which another takes pains with, improves, but runs the hazard of in husbandry."

True logic would have led them to reason forward from the truth they had determined; that there is no valid reason justifying interest on money. Resting on this truth, and then discovering that money may represent lands, the necessary conclusion must be, that land rentals are without justice. Reversing the order of their argument, they assumed a false premise, and from it attempted to prove true the very proposition they had found to be false.

There is the usury of lands as well as of "money or victuals."

Forty years ago the Omaha Indians went across the river and cut some fine grass growing on open land, and carried it to their reservation. The owner of the land, living in a distant state, learning of this, claimed pay of the Indians and brought suit against them before the agent to recover it. The Indians admitted that they had cut and taken the grass; they also admitted its value. Their defense was that this man had no right superior to theirs. This was a natural growth that had cost him no labor, and they had not injured the land. Their speaker said, "If the man had dug the land and planted it in corn and hoed and tended the corn, the corn would have been his; but the Great Spirit made the grass grow and this man gave it no labor nor care; the buffalo or the cattle could eat it. Have we not the rights of the cattle? This man has no right to it."

The agent decided against them and compelled them to pay the man. They were much dissatisfied and felt they were unjustly treated and oppressed, because they had to pay that which the man had never earned. The red men were not versed in legal statutes nor educated in the tutelage of usury, but it can not be denied that they interpreted very accurately the law written in the reason and conscience: that no man has any especial claim to that which he has not earned.

The convictions of white men, and their method of compelling absentee owners to pay for the increase in value of their lands, came under the writer's observation in a new settlement near the Indians' reservation. He found three poor families in a district. They had little land and extremely plain homes, but there was a good school-house and a good school and an expensive bridge had been built across a stream to enable one of the families to reach it. Enquiring how they could afford to erect such improvements and support such a school, they replied that the lands all around them were owned by absentees, speculators in the east, who were holding the lands for the advance in value, which they, in their struggling poverty, should make by the improvement of the country, when they would gather in an "unearned increment." They said they had the power to levy taxes for bridges and for schools and they had determined to make the absentees in this way compensate them, in part, for the increment they were earning for them.

The conviction of right and justice in the white settler did not differ from the innate and untutored argument of the Indian. The Indians felt oppressed because they were compelled to pay the man for what that man had never earned. The white settlers determined to thwart the purpose of the absentee owners to gain an increment from their sacrifice and labor.

The landlord has a right to all that he has produced. When he has cleared away the forest or broken up the land; when he has planted the vineyard and builded the winepress, he has a right to let this out to husbandmen to gather the fruits of his preparation and planting and to share with them in the proportion each has contributed to the production, but to hold all that he himself has produced and yet claim a part of the product of another, is usury. A farmer retires from his farm because no longer able or willing to continue its cultivation. He has an undisputed right to a full reward for all his own labor, and for all he has purchased from others that he leaves in the farm. There must be a compensation for the transformation of the wilderness into a farm at the first, for the fertility that may have been added to the soil, for the orchards, vineyards, houses, barns and every improvement he may have made and left on the farm. He has an undisputed right to all the labor remaining in the farm. If he sells he expects compensation for all this.

But if he sells, he must begin at once to consume its price, unless he becomes a usurer and is supported by the interest. If he does not sell, but retains his farm, he must also begin at once to consume the farm.

For him to demand of his tenant that the farm shall remain as valuable as when he left it, the soil not permitted to become less fertile, the buildings to be kept from decay and restored when destroyed, the orchards to be kept vigorous and young by the planting of new trees and vines; in short, the farm to be preserved in full value and yet pay a rental, is usury in land.

The preservation of a farm or land and its restoration to the owner unimpaired after a term of years involves far more than persons not informed suppose. It seems to them unreasonable to farm a field and only return the unimpaired field to the owner.

While land is stable and possibly the most easily preserved of all forms of property, at least a thief cannot carry it away, yet the preservation of land involves great care and risk.

The taking of any crop from any land reduces its fertility. On the virgin, western fertile lands the farmers laughed at the thought that they should ever need to return fertilizers, but it was only a few years until they yearned for the fertility they had extravagantly wasted. Buildings inevitably decay and they may be destroyed by fire or storm. Orchards may be overturned by a cyclone or be destroyed by blight or by the thousand enemies of the various varieties of fruit trees. The land may be injured by washing that may require years to repair. A single storm has destroyed fields in this way that never can be restored. Noxious weeds take possession of land that can only be eradicated by infinite pains. In this state certain weeds are declared outlaws and must be destroyed by the farmer for the protection of his neighbors. The farmer in this locality must have an alert eye for Canada thistles and oxeye daisy. It often causes more labor to eradicate them than the land is worth on which they are growing.

If the annual renter was required to give bond for the return of the farm unimpaired, returning that which the crops and time must consume and destroy, taking all risks of every character upon himself, a thoughtful man, though poor and needing the opportunity, would hesitate. It might involve him in an obligation he could not discharge in his whole life through conditions and providences over which he has no control.

Practically in this country the owner renting a farm from year to year does consume it. It begins at once to decline in fertility, the improvements begin to fall into decay, weeds take possession, washes occur and are not repaired, and in a few years the half of the value is gone. The owner is fortunate if he has received in rentals sufficient to restore its former value.

Under a system of perpetual tenantry the case is different. If the fertility declines it is the tenant's loss. The improvements are his and may be sold as one could sell ordinary farm tools, but not to be removed. If they are impaired or destroyed it does not affect the annual rental.

The landed proprietor in city or country, who has permanent tenants, who are required to make every improvement and keep up perfectly the fertility, and who pay an annual rental, is in the same class as those who are receiving annual interest. The landlord practically holds a perpetual mortgage, and the rental is the interest or increase exacted generation after generation.

The debtor working under a mortgage is cheered by the hope that he may be able, some day, to lift it, but the perpetual tenant on entailed lands knows that he is doomed to hopeless tenantry. He can never own the land and he is in the power of the landlord, who is often oppressive.

Calvin, in his letter of apology for usury of money, speaks of the injustice of the landlords in requiring a rental for "some barren farm" and of the "harsher" conditions imposed upon the tenants. Indeed his whole argument, when summed up, is, that the usury of lands is more cruel and oppressive than the usury of money.

While it is not yet true in America, yet considering the landlordships of Ireland and Great Britain and the older countries, with their unremitted exactions, grinding the life out of their tenants for a mere subsistence, it is likely that the race is today suffering more from the injustice and oppression of usury of land than from the usury of money.

The land question is too large for one short chapter or for one small book. It requires more and deeper study than the subject has ever yet received. The ownership of lands cannot be absolute; it must be limited by the rights of those who live upon them, but the limitations have never yet been clearly defined. If a man has a right to live he must have a right to a place to live. If a child has a right to be born it must have a right to a place to be born. It cannot be that the mass of our race only touch the earth by the sufferance of those who claim to own it.

The unprecedented rapidity of the development of this country is owing more to its wise and beneficent land laws than to anything else. They are not perfect but the most favorable to the landless that the world has ever known. No landlordism, no binding up lands by entail to make it forever impossible to gain a title to a portion of the soil, but our land laws, wisely devised, gave hope of a home to the homeless everywhere. The result was that our people from the eastern part of our own country, and the landless from across the seas, swarmed over the mountains and filled the Ohio valley and pushed on to the great Mississippi and Missouri valleys, and in three generations have transformed this waste into happy homes. The possession of land, of a home, ennobles the character, produces a patriotic love of this country and stimulates devotion to her institutions. The landless foreigner who makes here a home of his own is unwavering in his loyalty to the country of his adoption. Those foreigners, who do not fall in love with our institutions and do not become assimilated with our people, are tenants here as they were before they came here. They are not attached to our soil; they do not secure homes of their own and are therefore restless and a menace.

A dangerous tendency has been developing throughout our whole land in these later years. The usury of lands is on the increase. Tenantry is becoming more common on the farms in the country, while the mass of our city populations are living in rented houses or flats or crowded tenements.

The yearning for a home of one's own is deeply imbedded in human nature. To be denied the privilege of living in one's own house is one of the greatest trials of a life. This tendency to tenantry is not because our people have come to care less for a home of their own, but the conditions are not such as to make a purchase of a home profitable; the interest on the purchase price is greater than the usury of the land or rental. The natural and desirable state is for every family to own and occupy their home, and those conditions should be encouraged which make it unprofitable for any one to own real property he does not himself occupy, and which make it easy and profitable for every family to own their own home.

When all lands are owned by those who occupy them, the prophet Micah's picture of the millennial dawn will be realized. Every man shall sit under his own vine and under his own fig tree and no one shall molest him or make him afraid, by demanding a rental or by serving a writ of ejectment.

CHAPTER XXXV

PER CONTRA; POLITICAL ECONOMIST

The students of political economy are not always reformers. It is not their purpose nor the object of their studies to transform society. They only endeavor to explain why things are as they are. They find the taking of usury all but universal, and they endeavor to give the reasons for the prevailing custom. The subject is usually but slightly touched upon and dismissed with a few sentences.

Few economists claim that interest or rental is a part of the cost of production. They mostly affirm that it is no part of production; that it is merely the price paid for the opportunity to produce. The lender of money makes a loan to the borrower and thus gives him a better opportunity to produce than he had before. The landlord for the rental withdraws his hand from over his land and gives the renter the opportunity to produce a harvest.

In justification, or at least in explanation of this exaction for an opportunity, three reasons are usually given. These may be briefly stated as risk, time and abstinence.

1. There is some risk in every investment. There is a possibility that the most honest, industrious and careful debtor may by some misfortune not be able to return the loan and it would

therefore be lost. To guard against this the usurer requires the rate of interest to be graded by the measure of risk.

This is claimed to be of the nature of insurance, the borrower paying the premium. The profits of insurance are secured by collecting a larger premium than necessary to pay all losses. On this theory, the gain of usury is in the excess that can be secured of increase over the amounts lost.

This is the reverse of insurance. Insurance is the payment by an owner of property to a company who guarantees its preservation. Usury is the payment by the company to the owner for the privilege of guaranteeing that he shall not suffer loss.

Business involves a risk usually covered by insurance, but no honest man expects to make a profit out of his insurance.

2. A loan is made for a more or less extended time. Time is therefore claimed to be a ground for usury charges.

This claim rests on the assumption that time will increase wealth. But time is the great destroyer; time does not make gardens and farms, but covers them with weeds and sends them back to a wilderness; time does not erect a house, but pulls it down; time does not build a city, but causes it to crumble and a few ages buries it under the dust; time does not "incubate eggs, but turns them putrid; it does not transform into fowls. If eggs are developed into chickens the difference between eggs and chickens is the reward of the incubator."

Aside from the spirit of benevolence and sympathy with the needy there are three selfish reasons why a time loan may be made. First, the owner has no present need of it and wishes to be rid of its care. Second, the owner shall need it at a distant date and he wishes it preserved intact against that time. But these afford no ground for a charge of increase. He who stands and resists the ravages of time until the day it is needed does a positive service and deserves a reward. Third, the lender wishes to appropriate the earnings of another during the period of time given. This is the usurer's reason, and were it not for this time would lose its importance as an element; it is certain that long time loans would not be so attractive.

3. "The reward of abstinence" is a reward for refraining from consuming one's own wealth.

"You can not have your cake and eat it. If you do not eat it, you have your cake, but not a cake and a half. Not a cake and a quarter tomorrow, dunce, however abstinent you may be, only the cake you have, if the mice do not eat it in the night."— Ruskin.

The usual illustration is that of Jacob. He practiced abstinence in refraining from eating the bowl of pottage and giving it to his hungry brother. The reward of his abstinence was his brother's birthright.

If I do not take my soup now it is a great favor to have it preserved for me and served later, not cold and stale, but fresh and hot. If I deny myself now, for any cause, I can ask no more than that my meal shall be served, perfectly, later. This was all that Jacob could in justice demand of Esau.

It should be remembered, that because Jacob took Esau's birthright, as a reward of his abstinence, he was accounted a robber, was compelled to flee from his home, and not for twenty years see his father's face; that the consciousness of this sin and of the merited vengeance of the brother, whom he thereby defrauded and whom he thought was on his track, caused that night of struggle when he could not let the angel go, until he had his promise of deliverance.

Abstinence, to be benevolent, must be an act of personal loving self-sacrifice for another. Benevolent abstinence is its own reward and asks no more. Abstinence in hope of gain, denying himself while another is using his wealth, cannot be regarded as an act of benevolence, but of a selfish grovelling greed; more gratified to see his wealth increase than to himself enjoy its use. That is the spirit of the miser and receives the contempt of all right thinking people.

That the political economists are right in their analysis of the common thought of usury; that risk, time and abstinence are the elements of its basis in the popular mind, may not be denied, but if these are in fact the elements, then usury has no standing in equity and must be condemned by every enlightened conscience.

CHAPTER XXXVI

USURY IN HISTORY

It would require volumes to fully present the history of usury. A very brief summary must suffice in this place. Yet this synopsis may serve as a guide to those who may wish to pursue the investigation further and who have access to any considerable library of general and ecclesiastical history.

The exacting of usury has always been more or less practiced, and there has always been a contention against it as impolitic and wrong. In heathendom the philosophers and economists and common people were usually arrayed against it, and the voice of christendom has been practically unanimous in its denunciation until the 17th century. (For History of Usury in the Church, see Chapter X.)

Greece: Greece had no laws forbidding usury. The trade in money was left, like the trade in every thing else, without legal restraint. The law declared that the usurer should not demand a higher rate than that fixed by the original contract; it also advised "Let the usury on money be moderate." One per cent. per month was the usual rate.

There were among the Greeks at various times thoughtful men, who violently opposed the taking of increase. Solon, of aristocratic blood, but with strong sympathies for the oppressed classes, led a Nehemiah-like reformation. Solon was wise and patriotic. His name is a synonym for unselfish devotion to the public good. He was given authority in Greece in times of great financial distress. Debts were increasing. Mortgage stones were erected at the borders of each tract of land, giving the name of the creditor and the amount of his claim. The interest could not be paid. Interest taking had concentrated the wealth and power of the state in a few hands. The farmer lost all hope and was only a laborer on the farm he once owned. The debtor who had no farm to work for his creditor was yet in a worse condition; he was the mere slave of his creditor and could be sold by him. The free farmers were fast disappearing. The most of them were struggling with miserable poverty. Solon at once came to the relief of this suffering class. He released those who were enslaved and brought back those who had been sold abroad. The great work of Solon for this oppressed class has caused his name to be revered by all who have studied the history of his times.

Plato opposed usury, but he does not give extended reasons. Also the philosopher, Aristotle. His name is yet illustrious in the departments of natural and moral science and economics. With regard to usury he said: "Of all modes of accumulation, the worst and most unnatural is interest. This is the utmost corruption of artificial degeneracy; standing in the same relation to commerce that commerce does to economy. By commerce money is perverted from the purpose of exchange to that of gain; still this gain is occasioned by the mutual transfer of different objects; but interest, by transferring merely the same object from one hand to another generates money from money, and the product thus generated is called offspring (toxos) as being precisely the same nature as that from which it proceeds."

Rome: In the early ages of Rome there were no laws regulating the loans of money. The practice was common and was one of the most frequent subjects of popular complaint. In the celebrated secession of the lower classes of the people to Mons Sacer, when civil strife and fraternal bloodshed was threatened, the loudest outcry was against the oppression of exhorbitant interest exacted by wealthy citizens of those who were obliged to borrow. The common rate was twelve per cent. per annum. This is inferred from the fact that six per cent. was called half interest and three per cent. one-fourth interest.

The early records of Rome prove conclusively the odium attached to the business of money-lending for profit. In the codification of laws in the fifth century B.C. the rate of usury was fixed at one per cent. per month. This limitation of usury was enacted after a long and bitter contest between the rich lenders and the poorer classes.

A compromise seems to have been made in the assigned punishments. The laws for the collection of debts and the punishment of exacting more than the law permitted were alike extremely cruel.

The creditors of an insolvent debtor were given the power of cutting his body in pieces and the power of selling his children into slavery. The penalty of taking more than this legal interest was punished with more severity than theft. The thief must restore double, but the usurer must restore fourfold. This we learn from Cato's treatise on "Agriculture." Cato's own opinion of usury is shown in the answer which he made when he was asked what he thought of usury, his reply was, "What do you think of murder?"

Nearly a hundred years later the Licinian law forbade all increase. A little later we find the one-half of one per cent. permitted by law. Then under Sylla the legal rate is made three per cent. In the time of Antony and Cleopatra it is four per cent. For a time there was utter confusion and intolerably oppressive rates prevailed. Horace, in his Satires, speaks of one lending at sixty per cent. In the reign of Tiberius Cæsar, Rome was again shaken with another usury sedition, an uprising of the people against the usurers. The law was finally adjusted in the Justinian Code, by a compromise permitting six per cent. and severely restraining the exorbitant rates.

Three hundred and twenty-three years B.C., Livy speaks of a creditor who kept his debtor in irons, claiming, besides the debt, the interest which he exacted with greatest severity. It was soon after decreed that this cruelty should end and that no citizen should be placed in irons or sold into slavery for debt.

At the close of the republic the rate was twenty-four per cent.

England: In the earliest periods of which we have any records we find that the doctrine, that letting money to hire was sinful, prevailed universally over the island of Great Britain. It was the prevailing opinion that interest, or usury, as it was then called, was unjust gain, forbidden by divine law, and which a good Christian could neither receive nor pay. In common law the practice of taking increase was classed among the lowest crimes against public morals. So odious was it among Christians that the practice was confined almost wholly to the Jews, who did not exact usury of Jews but of the Christians.

The laws of King Alfred, about 900 A.D., directed that the effects of money-lenders upon usury should be forfeited to the king, their lands to the lords under whom they were held, and they should not be buried in consecrated ground.

By the laws of Edward the Confessor, about 1050 A.D., the usurer forfeited all his property and was declared an outlaw and banished from England. In the reign of Henry II, about the close of the twelfth century, the estates of usurers were forfeited at their death and their children were disinherited.

His successor, Richard I, was yet more severe, forbidding the usurers attending his coronation, nor would he protect them from mob violence.

During the thirteenth century the severities against the usurers were not relaxed. King John confiscated their gathered wealth without scruple. It is recorded that he exacted an enormous fine of a Jew in Bristol for his usuries, and when the Jew refused to pay he ordered one of his teeth to be drawn daily until he should pay. The Jew is said to have endured the pulling of seven, but then weakened and paid the fine.

Henry III was equally harsh and severe in his measures. He exacted all he could and then turned them over to the Earl of Cornwall. "The one flayed and the other emboweled." It is written in the chronicles of England, 1251 A.D., "By such usurers and licentious liurs as belong to him, the realme had alreadie become sore corrupted."

In the fourteenth century, under the three Edwards, the taking of interest was an indictable offence and Edward III made it a capital crime.

In the fifteenth century, under Henry VII, the penalty was fixed at one hundred pounds and the penalty of the church added, which was excommunication.

Attorney General Noy, in the reign of James I, thought the taking of money by usury was no better than taking a man's life. He said: "Usurers are well ranked with murderers."

In the sixteenth century, under Henry VIII, it was enacted that all interest above ten per cent. was unlawful. Less was not collectable by law, but was not a punishable offence.

Edward VI revived the old laws condemning all interest.

Mary I, next following, executed these laws with extreme severity.

Elizabeth restored the laws of Henry VIII, in which usury less than ten per cent. was not a punishable offence. This edict of Elizabeth adds: "In the interpretation of the law it shall be largely and strongly construed for the repression of usury."

This law of Henry VIII and Elizabeth, with the rate of interest reduced, was the statute law of England until 1854, when all the usury laws were repealed.

In 1694 William and Mary II entered into a contract to secure a permanent loan and pledged the kingdom to pay interest on it forever.

The loan marked the turning point in the popular mind with regard to usury. As it was approved in their necessity by the king and queen at the head of the Protestant world, ecclesiastics began to shift their ground and to apologize for, and excuse, that which had been formerly unequivocably condemned. As the crown was the head of both the church and the state, the condemnation of usury seemed tinged both with disloyalty and heresy. The courts too began to modify their decisions to bring them into harmony with the action of the crown.

The change in the usury laws were not made by enactments of Parliament, but by the decisions of courts. The precedents were gradually accumulated and the statutes were merely made to conform to them.

CHAPTER XXXVII

FRANCIS BACON

From the short dissertation on usury found in the works of Bacon we learn that the taking of usury was a recognized evil and odious in his time.

It will be noticed that he eliminates risk from usury and sees that "In the game of certainties against uncertainties" usury is sure to win. It will be noticed also that he mentions only economic arguments against usury. He does not give ethical and moral reasons. He does not mention the want of sympathy for the poor and their oppression.

In his statement of the arguments in defence he implies that the usurer is less grasping than the man he knew who said "The devil take this usury."

This is the very opposite of the picture of the usurer given by his contemporary, Shakespeare, in his character, Shylock.

His specious argument for the regulation of the evil "For some small matter for the license" is familiar to modern reformers in connection with other sins. He speaks of the reduction of the usury rates as a general good and believes "It will no whit discourage the lender." Wrong-doers in all the ages have been ready to part with a portion of the profits of an unlawful business for the cover of the authority of the state.

The following is his discussion in full

247

1. OF USURY.

"Many have made witty invectives against usury. They say that it is a pity the devil should have God's part, which is the tithe. That the usurer is the greatest Sabbath breaker, because his plough goeth every Sunday. That the usurer is the drone that Virgil speaketh of:

"Ignavum fucos pecus a praesepibus arcent.

"That the usurer breaketh the first law that was made for mankind after the fall, which was, *in sudore vultus tui comedes panem tuum; non in sudore vultus alieni*; (in the sweat of thy face shalt thou eat bread—not in the sweat of another's face.) That usurers should have orange-tawney bonnets, because they do Judaize. That it is against nature for money to beget money; and the like. I say only this, that usury is a *concessum propter duritiem cordis*; (a thing allowed by reason of the hardness of men's hearts): for since there must be borrowing and lending, and men are so hard of heart as they will not lend freely, usury must be permitted. Some others have made suspicious and cunning propositions of banks, discovery of men's estates and other inventions. But few have spoken of usury usefully. It is good to set before us the incommodities and the commodities of usury, that the good may be either weighed out or culled out; and warily to provide, that while we make forth to that which is better, we meet not with that which is worse.

"The discommodities of usury are, first, it makes fewer merchants. For were it not for this lazy trade of usury, money would not lie still, but would in great part be employed upon merchandising; which is the *vena porta* of wealth in a state. The second, that it makes poor merchants. For as a farmer can not husband his ground so well if he sit at a great rent, so the merchant can not drive his trade so well, if he sit at great usury.

The third is incident to the other two; and that is the decay of customs of kings or states, which ebb or flow with merchandising. The fourth that it bringeth the wealth or treasure of a realm or state into a few hands.

"For the usurer being at certainties, and others at uncertainties, at the end of the game most of the money will be in the box; and ever a state flourisheth when wealth is more equally spread. The fifth that it beats down the price of land; for the employment of money is chiefly either purchasing or merchandising; and usury waylays both. The sixth, that it doth dull and damp all industries, improvements and new inventions, wherein money would be stirring, if it were not for this slug. The last, that it is the canker and ruin of many men's estates; which in process of time breeds a public poverty.

"On the other side, the commodities of usury are, first, that howsoever usury in some respect hindereth merchandising, yet in some other it advanceth it; for it is certain that the greatest part of trade is driven by young merchants upon borrowing at interest; so as if the usurer either call in or keep back his money, there will ensue presently a great stand of trade. The second is, that were it not for this easy borrowing upon interest, man's necessities would draw upon them a most sudden undoing; in that they would be forced to sell their means (be it lands or goods) far under foot; and so, whereas usury doth but gnaw upon them, bad markets would swallow them quite up. As for mortgaging or pawning, it will little mend the matter; for either men will not take pawns without use; or if they do, they will look precisely for the forfeiture. I remember a cruel monied man in the country that would say: 'The devil take this usury, it keeps us from forfeitures of mortgages and bonds.' The third and last is, that it is a vanity to conceive that there would be ordinary borrowing without profit; and it is impossible to conceive the number of inconveniences that would ensue if borrowing be cramped. Therefore, to speak of the abolishing of usury is idle. All states have ever had it, in one kind or rate, or other. So as that opinion must be sent to Utopia.

"To speak now of the reformation and reiglement of usury; how the discommodities of it may be best avoided, and the commodities of it retained. It appears by the balance of commodities and discommodities of usury, two things are to be reconciled. The one, that the tooth of usury be grinded that it bite not too much; the other, that there be left open a means to invite monied men to lend to the merchants for the continuing and quickening of trade. This can not be done except you introduce two several sorts of usury, a less and a greater. For if you reduce usury to one low rate it will ease the common borrower, but the merchant will be to seek for money. And it is to be noted, that the trade of merchandise, being the most lucrative, may bear usury at a good rate: other contracts not so.

"To serve both intentions, the way would be briefly thus: That there be two rates of interest; the one free and general for all, the other under license only, to certain persons and in certain places of merchandising. First, therefore, let usury in general be reduced to five in the hundred; and let that rate be proclaimed free and current; and, let the state shut itself out to take any penalty for the same. This will preserve borrowing from any general stop or dryness. This will ease infinite borrowers in the country. This will, in great part, raise the price of land, because land purchased at sixteen years' purchase will yield six in the hundred and somewhat more; whereas this rate of interest yields but five. This, by like reason, will encourage and edge industrious and profitable improvements; because many will rather venture in that kind than take five in the hundred, especially having been used to greater profit. Secondly, let there be certain persons licensed to lend to known merchants upon usury at a higher rate; and let it be with the cautions following: Let the rate be, even with the merchant himself, somewhat more easy than that he used formerly to pay; for by that means all borrowers shall have some ease by this reformation, be he merchant or whosoever. Let it be bank or common stock, but every man be master of his own money. Not that I altogether mislike banks, but they will hardly be brooked in regard of certain suspicions. Let the state be answered some small matter for the license, and the rest left to the lender; for if the abatement be but small, it will no whit discourage the lender. For he, for example, that took before ten or nine in the hundred, will sooner descend to eight in the hundred than give over his trade in usury, and go from certain gains to gains of hazard. Let these licensed lenders be in number indefinite, but restrained to certain principal cities and towns of merchandising; for then they will be hardly able to color other men's monies in the country. So as the license of nine will not suck away the current rate of five; for no man will lend his monies far off, nor put them into unknown hands.

"If it be objected that this doth in a sort authorize usury, which before was in some places but permissive; the answer is, that it is better to mitigate usury by declaration, than to suffer it to rage by connivance."

2.   (Works of Francis Bacon, Vol. 12, Page 218.)

CHAPTER XXXVIII

WHY THIS TRUTH WAS NEGLECTED

That we may find the way of return, we must consider the reasons of our wandering. We must reverse our direction and retrace our steps. These reasons are not occult or hard to find.

1. The departure had its root in man's depraved nature. The natural tendency is evil, while the graces must be cultivated with great diligence. Evils grow as weeds grow in the garden, as thorns and thistles and briers cover the untended fields. This evil has not been disturbed by any book exposing its harm for a hundred years, and it has been two hundred since it was treated as a violation of the Eighth Commandment. This evil, thus left undisturbed, has flourished and spread over all the world.

2. Two and three hundred years ago the great doctrines were occupying the thought of Christendom. The doctrines of free grace, by repentance and an exercise of faith, were receiving close attention. The creeds of the denominations were being unfolded, and their defense and proof absorbed the thought of the wise and good. What shall we believe was the question?

3. Other great evils stood before the faces of those who labored for the uplifting of the race. Practices attached to the ecclesiastics, and degrading the organized church, were flaunted before the eyes of those who stood for true faith and pure

living. These were attacked with vigor, while this evil, which had been especially the sin of the Jew, crept in and entrenched itself.

4. Covetousness is one of those secret sins that may lurk in the heart while there is maintained a fair outward life. Few will admit this sin. Priests declare that this is the one sin that is never voluntarily confessed. Usury is the common outward activity of this inward state, and when usury was made lawful by the statutes of the realm, the voice of conscience was silenced. The conscience that would cry out in protest against a rate of interest forbidden by law, will permit the same rate when the statutes of the state are changed.

5. Early education and natural buoyancy have led the debtors to be less sensitive to the burdens of usury upon them.

A large portion of our present arithmetic is taken up with percentage. The position of the student, in mind, is that of the creditor. This is presumed in the statements of the problems and lies in the thought of the student in all the calculations. If the statements of propositions and their conclusions were made to place the student on the debtor side, then the study of percentage would educate him to a horror of this sin.

When a loan is made, the attention of the borrower is seldom called to the rapidity of increase and the dangers of accumulation. If this were done, and a prompt return of both principal and interest required, at the end of the term the borrower would soon be alarmed at the hopelessness of permanent gain through debt.

Peter Cooper, it is said, taught this lesson to a friend who was talking of borrowing for six months at three per cent. We clip the following story:

"Why do you borrow money for so short a time?" Mr. Cooper asked.

"Because the brokers will not negotiate bills for longer."

"Well, if you wish," said Mr. Cooper, "I will discount your note at that rate for three years."

"Are you in earnest?" asked the would-be borrower.

"Certainly I am. I will discount your note for ten thousand dollars for three years at that rate. Will you do it?"

"Of course I will," said the merchant.

"Very well," said Mr. Cooper. "Just sign this note for ten thousand dollars, payable in three years, and give me your check for eight hundred dollars, and the transaction will be complete."

"But where is the money for me?" asked the astonished merchant.

"You don't get any money," was the reply. "Your interest for thirty-six months at three per cent. per month amounts to one hundred and eight per cent., or ten thousand eight hundred dollars. Therefore, your check for eight hundred dollars just makes us even."

There has come to this table, a letter recently sent by a wise uncle to his nephew, who sought from him his first loan. Usually the interest is minimized while the hopeful youth is permitted to indulge his dreams of fancied good, to be easily gained by a loan.

"My Near Nephew:

"I enclose a draft for forty dollars with a note for the amount to me, due in one year at six per cent., which please sign and return to me. This is probably the first note that you have ever given, and there are one or two things about a note that maybe you have never discovered. One striking peculiarity is, that they always come due, though they are drawn for a year. It may seem a long time, but when you have a note come due at the end of the year it seems altogether too short and has gone before you are aware of it. Another peculiar thing is, that while interest is a little thing apparently, yet it never works on the eight-hour system, but continues steadily through the whole twenty-four, and through the whole seven days in the week. Its about the most industrious animal of my acquaintance, working nights and Sundays as well, and apparently never becoming in the least fatigued, consequently, though it appears to be so slow, still if you do not watch it closely, the first thing you know you will be astonished at what an amount of work it has accomplished. There are other things equally striking about notes, but these two are the most important, and the ones I particularly wish to impress on your mind.

"_____

"P.S.—Don't think from the tone of this that I'm not willing to let you have the money. I merely want to impress on you what it means to go in debt."

6. The evil was not hitherto so much felt. This, especially, is true in the United States. Great natural resources, unclaimed wealth, made the burden of a small debt unfelt. By appropriating the vast unbroken forests and untilled lands and unopened mines of precious metals, of coal and iron and gas and oil, there seemed such evident advantages from the borrowed capital that the evils were unnoticed, until these natural resources had been appropriated and were held in private hands, and the opportunities are found to be denied those who have come so closely after.

This system made it possible for one generation to grasp a continent; to grasp all its natural resources and hold them, and compel tribute from all that came after. Taking only a limited and short-time view, the advantages seemed great and the evils small. But looking at the welfare of the generations its evils might have been clearly discerned.

7. The evil was never before so great. The vast accumulations of wealth, so sure to follow the operation of usury, was hitherto unknown. Corporations, combinations for the handling of great interests, grasping the natural resources and monopolizing the natural wealth, gaining franchises covering a monopoly of privileges in transportation, light and communication by the telephone or telegraph, are comparatively recent.

8. The first appearance of indebtedness is a seeming, but false, prosperity. The young man who takes possession of a tract of land and then, with borrowed capital, improves it, building his house and his barns and his permanent buildings, and stocking it with animals that please his taste, has the appearance of abounding prosperity, but as the unending grind of usury continues, these, he comes to feel, are but weights to which he is chained, and in an agony of sweat he is compelled to wear out his life.

A city incurring debt is seemingly prosperous. Bonds are issued for the erection of attractive public buildings, for the paving of muddy streets, for the beautifying of public parks. These bond issues are signs of the prosperity of only one class, the usurers. The ultimate burden is upon the laborers, who must pay every bond, interest and principal.

9. The opponents of usury have not always been wise. They have indulged in bitter invective rather than solid argument. The language of the fathers, especially, was unqualified in severity.

257

When the absurdity and unmitigated evil of usury is seen, and one feels that adequacy requires superlatives, it is not easy to restrain language and use mild terms. The divine prohibition was so clear and the effects so oppressive, especially to the poor, that it did not appear to the fathers to require argument. The divine authority was not, therefore, followed up with the economic basis or reasons for the prohibitions.

Usury crept in because it was not barred out by the sound reasoning of those who knew its evils. The vituperations were ignored as the rantings of ill-balanced minds.

10. Like every other wrong, it feeds upon itself. The very conditions it produces fosters and promotes its growth. At first directing effort and thought along material lines, ultimately the ideals become groveling. The purposes of a worthy life and the characteristics of a noble manhood are perverted. There comes a wrong idea of true greatness. There arises a false measure of manhood. That measure is wealth, and of all the grounds of distinction among men, wealth is the most sordid. Success is accumulation of wealth. Prosperity is getting rich. Whatever else a man may accomplish in life, if he remains poor he is accounted a failure. Yet to this pass, such a pass, have we come, that our national and age characteristic is that of material gain, commonly called commercialism. This was not the thought of our fathers who subordinated material gain to the development of noble manhood. This is a perversion of our American traditions, and is a menace to better development of the individual and of the state.

11. Wrong laws mislead the judgment and pervert the conscience. If there is a want of harmony between the moral and statute law when selfish interests are served, the moral law will be ignored. State laws ease the conscience that would be otherwise troubled. The rate of usury fixed by a state is used as a moral guide. When the legal rate is six per cent. it is wrong to take eight, but when the legal rate is ten per cent. then it is not

wrong to take ten. The familiarity of our people with laws recognizing and enforcing interest rates has perverted their ideas of right and justice by substituting the statute for the divine moral law. But state laws can also trouble the conscience that is at ease and be a teacher of righteousness. Let the ancient laws forbidding usury be placed upon our statute books and enforced, and it would not be half a generation till the conscience and reason both approved.

Nothing in history more shocked the conscience of Christendom than the compact of William and Mary with usurers in 1694. That was in direct conflict with the teachings and practice of all the ages among Christians. It has taken two hundred years for courts and states and financial institutions to first dull the Christian conscience and then secure its approval. The world now awaits the coming of some captain of righteousness, equal in authority and influence in church and state, who will organize a return to the faith and practice of the fathers.

CHAPTER XXXIX

CRUSHED TRUTH
WILL RISE AGAIN

The practice of usury is so general, and it is apparently so fully approved and sanctioned by many of the most intelligent and virtuous of our people, that those who believe in its prohibition and are disposed to pessimism may be utterly discouraged.

Truth must eventually prevail. Any custom or system built upon falsehood must sooner or later yield. The house built upon the sand must in time fall. It may be undermined by years of instruction and so gradually give way that the date of its overthrow can hardly be determined, or it may in its strength be taken in a storm and fall. The whole commercial credit system built on this monstrous falsehood must either crumble or tumble.

The prophet Isaiah was hopeful and happy in the midst of the most unfavorable conditions of corruption and alienation from the truth, for he was able with his prophetic eye to catch a glimpse of the good time coming, when righteousness should completely triumph. "He shall teach us of His ways and we shall walk in His steps." "With righteousness shall He judge the poor." "Righteousness shall be the girdle of His loins."

No prophet has fixed a date for the suppression of usury, yet no intelligent man of faith, familiar with the reforms of the past, when as thoroughly entrenched and as giant evils were attacked and overthrown, need be in despair.

We were enslaved by superstitions. Haunted houses were numerous and the bewitching of people was frequent. Two hundred arrests for witchcraft were made in a single year, 1692, and twenty of these persons were put to death. These persecutions were urged and defended by Cotton Mather, a representative of the highest intelligence and culture of the times. His mother was a daughter of John Cotton, and his father the President of Harvard College. Now black cats and epilepsy inspire no fear, and ghost stories do not now terrify and unnerve our children.

Duelling prevailed among men of honor. Public opinion made it compulsory that personal differences between gentlemen should be settled in this way. Persons were branded as cowards who would not put their lives in jeopardy. Few had the courage to resist. Duels were common among the political leaders at Washington. Many a shot rang out at sunrise in the little valley at Bladensburg, the noted duelling ground. Jackson and Benton and Clay and De Witt Clinton were duellists. After the killing of Alexander Hamilton by Aaron Burr, in 1804, the whole country was aroused and an agitation began against the custom, but it yielded slowly. In 1838 and 1841 there were duels between distinguished congressmen. But now public opinion is so transformed that the "honorable and brave" duellist is a moral coward.

Gambling was a common sin. There were lotteries organized for the raising of funds for state and municipal expenses. There were raffles at church fairs to support the ordinances in the sanctuary. The rules of the games were protected by the laws of the state. No one who had lost in a game could recover by law unless he proved that the rules of the game had not been followed. The rules for gambling were regarded as legitimate as the regulations of any business. The gambler was only a law-breaker when he "cheated." Now gambling is unlawful in every state and territory, and any newspaper advertising a lottery is shut out of our mails. Even an "honest" gambler is now classed among robbers.

Intemperance was rampant through the eighteenth century and more than half the nineteenth. Whisky was king. Through a false physiology it became the almost universal opinion that in the great portion of the United States the climate required the use of "ardent spirit." Ministers and all classes of the people were thus deluded, and almost every person, adult or child, was a consumer.

"Upon rising in the morning a glass of liquor must be taken to give an appetite for breakfast. At eleven o'clock the merchant in his counting-room, the blacksmith at his forge, the mower in the hay field, took a dram to give them strength till the ringing of the bell or the sounding of the horn for dinner. In mid-afternoon they drank again. When work for the day was done, before going to bed, they quaffed another glass. It was the regular routine of drinking in well-regulated and temperate families. Hospitalities began with drinking. 'What will you take?' was the question of host to visitor. Not to accept the proffered hospitality was disrespectful. Was there the raising of a meeting house, there must be hospitality for all the parish: no lack of liquor; and when the last timber was in its place a bottle of rum must be broken upon the ridge-place. In winter men drank to keep themselves warm; in summer to keep themselves cool; on rainy days to keep out the wet, and on dry days to keep the body in moisture. Friends, meeting or parting, drank to perpetuate their friendship. Huskers around the corn-stack, workmen in the field, master and apprentice in the shop, passed the brown jug from lip to lip. The lawyer drank before writing his brief or pleading at the bar; the minister, while preparing his sermon or before delivering it from the pulpit. At weddings bridegroom, bride, groomsman, and guest quaffed sparkling wines. At funerals minister, friend, neighbor, mourner, all except the corpse, drank of the bountiful supply of liquors always provided. Not to drink was disrespectful to living and dead, and depriving themselves of comfort and consolation. In every community there were blear-eyed men with bloated, haggard faces; weeping women, starving children." (Building of a Nation. Page 271.)

While "temperate" men were grieved at the tide of wretchedness and protested, they did not think it possible to get on without whisky. Dr. Prime, for so many years editor of the New York Observer, told of the meeting of the family physician and the pastor at his father's home in a case of severe illness. When the physician took his leave the pastor followed him into the yard, where they had a long consultation. The pastor was anxiously seeking advice. Three drinks made his head swim, and the problem was how he could make more than three calls and not become unsteady. The doctor gave directions and Dr. Prime said that neither the minister nor the physician thought of the simple remedy, "not drinking."

It has taken two generations, but the transformation is marvelous. The minister can now call in every home in his parish and never once have an opportunity to drink. If Rev. John Pierpont was yet living, who was put out of his pulpit in Boston by an ecclesiastical council because he publicly protested against the use of the basement of his church as a storeroom for whisky, he would see every minister losing his pulpit who would not publicly protest against such a desecration. Rev. George B. Cheever, the dreamer, in 1830, woke up the stupid consciences of the fuddled men and women; he wrote out his dream and published it, "Deacon Giles' Distillery," and went to jail for it, but even he never dreamed of the greatness of the temperance reform that has followed.

The overthrow of chattel slavery is complete and the human rights of the inferior peoples are recognized. Human slavery was of old, as ancient as history; it was widespread over the world; there was an immense and profitable commerce in human flesh; luxurious wealth and ease was secured by appropriating labor without compensation; it was thought that the Scriptures in both Testaments approved the holding of bondmen; there was a consciousness of superior gifts; there was a firm belief that the negroes, especially, needed the care of the superior race; that they were better off and happier than they would be in freedom; there was a deep-seated race prejudice that remains unyielding till this day. Yet the slave trade has ceased, stopped by armed vessels patroling the seas. The slaves, eight hundred thousand, in the West Indies were set free; the shackles were stricken off by the sword in the United States; Brazil adopted gradual emancipation, and chattel slavery disappeared forever from the civilized world.

The reform battles fought and won are assurances that victory shall also reward those who contend against this sin of usury. There are also other good grounds for confidence.

1. They are seeking only a return—a reform: "a restoration to a former state;" they are not seeking for the establishment of some new and untried theory, but they are seeking a return to the faith and conduct of the righteous from the beginning and up seventeen centuries of the Christian era. The race is but temporarily deflected to the worship of the golden calf.

2. There is coming forward a great army of intelligent, virtuous young people. They are made intelligent by our high schools, seminaries and colleges. They are made students of the Bible and stimulated in righteousness by Sunday Schools, Christian Associations, Endeavors, Leagues and Unions. From these there shall rise up defenders of the truth, free from the burden of debt and unbiassed by life-long association with conditions familiar to those older. The reformers in all ages have been young, and this reform will be no exception. There is a rashness in youth that needs direction, but there is also a dash and hope

and confidence that is necessary to break away from old customs. One generation of intelligent, virtuous young people could give this evil its fatal blow.

Usury cannot flourish among the vicious and the unreliable. Other evils may flourish among the idle, the indolent, the treacherous, the deceitful and the dishonest, but industry and economy and integrity and faithfulness and honor and even God-fearing piety are desirable qualities in the usurer's victims. The higher the civilization, yes Christian civilization, the more is produced and the richer the harvest. The usurer has no use for a savage. This worm thrives in the living body and sucks its vitality. It cannot flourish in putrid flesh. Let the highest types of our young manhood avoid this sin and its death knell is sounded.

3. Present conditions stimulate an interest in this question. The unequal distribution of the vast wealth now being produced: the earnings of the many turned into the coffers of a few; the struggles between the employers and their employees; organized labor and combinations of wealth; lead to a closer study of this and allied economic questions than they have ever received before. The solution of these questions will expose the fraud of usury.

4. The patriotic spirit has not decayed in our people and rulers. They are as strongly attached to our free, popular institutions as were the patriots of '76. There is alarm at the tendency to slip away from the early traditions, at the centralization of power, at class legislation. The influence of usury is so strong to promote a favored class and to concentrate power, that it must be resisted as an enemy to our republican institutions. It gradually undermined and then destroyed the republic of Venice, and it is now doing its first work with us. It must soon emerge from its cover. Then our people will arouse with their patriotic fervor and fell it with one blow, and then bury it with the other enemies of the government that have from time to time arisen.

5. In the studies in sociology there is now a strong current toward Socialism. There is a desire to preserve the individual's interests and yet a stronger disposition to merge him in the general welfare.

There is a conviction that the privileges of individuals have been unduly guarded while the rights of the public were neglected, that the rights of individuals have received an excess of protection while the welfare of the great mass of the people has been sacrificed. The present problem of the student of sociology is, How can the rights of individuals be adjusted, yet so as to maintain the superior interests of all the people? This can be accomplished largely, if not completely, by the abolition of usury.

Let the Government receive on deposit the surplus wealth of the individuals for safe keeping and subject to their orders. Let the Postal Savings Bank be established. The Government is the best possible security. The certificates of deposit would be as good as Government bonds. They could take the place of the National Bank currency. The Postal Department now transfers money and in a manner receives deposits and issues postal notes.

These deposits as they accumulated would lift from the people the burden of the interest bearing debt. As they increased the Government could invest them in public utilities to be operated for the general welfare. The Government thus caring for the surplus wealth the people are entitled to any benefits that may accrue from its use. All would have an interest in preserving and all would share in the advantages of the property thus cared for by the State, while each would have his individual earnings subject to draft for his personal needs or pleasure.

This would preserve the rights of the individual and secure to him perfectly his surplus earnings, and at the same time the whole people, through the Government, would have the use of this accumulated wealth for its safe-keeping. This will preserve the stimulating incentives of individualism and also gain, practically, the blessings of Socialism. This will be the natural conclusion in the balancing and adjustment of the present sociological discussion.

6. The prohibition of usury would be to the material advantage of the great mass of our people. It would be a blessing to all, though it might hinder the material gain of a few, but the hindered would not be a tithe of our people. It is not easy to forsake the wrong when appetite or passion or selfish interests plead for it. The martyrs who will stand by the right "though the heavens fall" are not a majority of our people. The paths of righteousness are easy, broad and smooth, and crowded with enthusiastic shouters when self-interest can walk hand in hand with a reform. Opposition to usury is self-defense to the poor, the pensioners, the producers, and they form a mighty, irresistible army.

7. Reason remains. The laws of logic have not changed nor has the human mind lost its power of tracing premises to their conclusion. The custom of usury was never reasoned into practice, but was permitted to creep in while reason was diverted to abstract, abstruse, scholastic subjects by those who claimed to be scholars. Had the fathers reasoned more about practical subjects, and scolded less, this sin would never have appeared in Christian society and claimed respectability. When the people begin to think and to turn their reasoning powers to this subject, as light dispels darkness, this gross error will flee away.

8. The conscience is yet alert to condemn the wrong and to approve the right. The public conscience was never more tender nor more delicately adjusted, but it is wanting in intelligence in this matter. The eye cannot see to determine the nature of an object without light, so the conscience must be enlightened, or made intelligent by the reason, to enable it to

give a right decision. Conscience is the same in all ages among all peoples, and when informed by investigation and reasoning, the condemnation of usury will be as unanimous as in the centuries of the past.

Prayer is also a means to this righteous end. God is still on His throne. His ear is not heavy. He hears the cry of the raven and sparrows and lions. He hears the cry of His suffering children and will not fail to come to their relief. In all the past, man's extremity has been God's opportunity. Relief has come at unexpected times and by ways that were not known. Sometimes by means that were insignificant and inadequate in order to show that it was not by human might or power; sometimes by the faith of one humble believer.

This writer has been familiar with the story of David and Goliath from his infancy. To him, Mammon, whose head is usury, is the giant Philistine who now stalks forth to defy "the armies of the living God," and with a grain of David's faith, he flings this stone.

CALVIN ELLIOTT